PRAISE FOR *THE TANGIBLE KINGDOM*

"Hugh Halter and Matt Smay are not just men of words but of actions. They have broken from the pack of theorizers, philosophers, and abstract theologians by diving into the deeper waters of experimentation, struggle, failure, and success. The results are sharper principles packed with punch because they have been refined in the fires of real life. Take confidence that what they teach will work."—**Neil Cole**, church starter, director of Church Multiplication Associates, author of *Organic Church*

"Hugh and Matt are real live heroes, not only because they provide some original insights into the nature of the mission of incarnational ways of church, but because they courageously pave the way for the rest of us to follow. Laced with the inspirational authority that only practitioners can provide, this book deserves to be taken seriously by all concerned with mission and church in the twenty-first century."—**Alan Hirsch** (theforgottenways.com), author of *The Forgotten Ways* and *The Shaping of Things to Come* (with Mike Frost), founding director of Forge Mission Training Network

"In *The Tangible Kingdom* we are given a picture of hope that the church really needs right now. Do you want your church to become a community of incarnation that displays the Kingdom throughout the world? Are you humble enough to admit you don't know how? Then you need to read this book. Finally someone is telling us how to do that very thing."—**Rick McKinley**, pastor of Imago Dei Community, author of *This Beautiful Mess* and *Jesus in the Margins*

"I have spent my adult life in church planting, evangelism, and church consultation. I've had hundreds of conversations with totally sincere people trying to crack the code of "what it really means to plant a missional church." I could sense some directions in which we needed to move, but I was always simultaneously aware of big holes in my thinking—and even bigger holes in my experience base. Thankfully Hugh and Matt have filled the gap. This is the most real-storied, coherent, and practical book I have read on the subject."—**Todd Hunter**, national director, Alpha USA

"Plunging deeper and deeper with Jesus into a grassroots incarnational life is what this book is about. Many aspire to it, some write about it, but very few live out the rhythms of such a holistic lifestyle in the way that Hugh and Matt and their families are currently doing. I am thrilled to see their journey in book form."—**Andrew Jones**, tallskinnykiwi.com

"I don't need another book to tell me that the cultural currents of our time have shifted and the church is floundering in uncharted waters. That's as clear as the nose on your face. What I need are practical, biblical, tried-and-tested steps to piloting the church through these shifting currents. In Halter and Smay you have practitioners who aren't just holding on for grim death in the midst of rough seas. They are riding the shifting cultural swells, surfing the rising waves, and having a ball doing it! Written by experienced church planters who love what they do, *The Tangible Kingdom* is a navigational guide for the stout-hearted missional leader.—**Michael Frost**, author, *Exiles* and *The Shaping of Things to Come*

"In the rapidly secularizing environment of the post-modern West, there are a myriad of voices trying to give guidance to existing or potential followers of Jesus, many of whom are perplexed and disoriented. This volume is a clear voice. It is accurate, inspirational, and most importantly, written by practitioners and not theorists."—**Sam Metcalf**, president of Church Resource Ministries

"Taking from the past to define the present, Hugh Halter and Matt Smay are not just thought-leaders of exceptional ability but leading practitioners of missional communities and innovative congregational forms. This book is a roadmap of the future."—**Eric Swanson**, Leadership Network, co-author of *The Externally Focused Church*

"The Kingdom of God alive among us, that is what we all want. And that is what Hugh and Matt give us in *The Tangible Kingdom*. Be not fooled into thinking that "tangible" means simple, or one-size fits all. In this delightfully helpful book we are reminded that tangible means real-life. This is a book that reminds us and calls us to a faith with real-world implications."—**Doug Pagitt**, author of *A Christianity Worth Believing*

"As someone who has been in this field for thirty-plus years, I can say with confidence: this is the direction of the future of the church. Missional, incarnational ministry gives hands and feet to the body of Christ in ways that communicate the profound reality of Jesus to the world. Hugh and Matt have stripped ministry back down to the early church essentials, and rooted it in a strong Christology.—**Bob Logan**, president, CoachNet International Ministries

"Written with honesty, humor, and a deeply felt hope for the body of Christ, *The Tangible Kingdom* will be an essential resource in helping people discover their own answers for what the church can look like. Whether you serve an established congregation or are in the process of starting something new, you'll find inspiration here for your ministry. You'll find a church that's not about form but about function."—**Bob Logan**, president of CoachNet International Ministries

"*The Tangible Kingdom* is a guide that leads us into a new vision for church without making us feel guilty for not knowing about it earlier. It takes the mystery out of missional and makes it practical and doable. You may not want to be a Christian when you get done reading, but you will definitely want to follow Christ."—**Jim Henderson**, author of *Jim and Casper Go to Church*

"This is a book about seeking the Kingdom of God relentlessly in a world of fractured journeys and dead-ended good intentions. With Kingdom eyes, Hugh and Matt glimpse possibilities for the church that inspire me and can help set Christian leaders free to imagine and explore."—**John Hayes**, Director of InnerChange, author of "*Submerge.*"

"This is a book that will take you where you to need to go if you have any kind of future care for the church. Within my sixty-five years I've witnessed many shifts, and trends come and go like the ever-changing breeze. A clearer, radical, life-transforming focus that has been tested and tried according to the ways of Jesus has been desperately needed. *The Tangible Kingdom* provides that focus. This is a book of hope for the future of the church, and anyone who dares to lead within it. This book will bring the honest clarity and focus and encouragement your soul has been longing for as you seek to be a part of a community of faith that will impact the world God's way . . . missionally, realistically, tangibly, incarnationally . . . forever."—**Wes Roberts**, co-author of *Reclaiming God's Original Intent for the Church*

The Tangible Kingdom

Creating Incarnational Community

THE POSTURE AND PRACTICES
OF ANCIENT CHURCH NOW

Hugh Halter and Matt Smay

Foreword by Reggie McNeal

A LEADERSHIP NETWORK PUBLICATION

JOSSEY-BASS
A Wiley Imprint
www.josseybass.com

Published by Jossey-Bass
A Wiley Imprint
989 Market Street, San Francisco, CA 94103-1741   www.josseybass.com

Jossey-Bass books and products are available through most bookstores. To contact Jossey-Bass directly call our Customer Care Department within the U.S. at 800-956-7739, outside the U.S. at 317-572-3986, or fax 317-572-4002.

Scripture quotations are from *New American Standard Bible: 1995 update*. 1995 (Ac 16:16). LaHabra, CA: The Lockman Foundation and *The Holy Bible: New International Version*. 1996, c1984. Grand Rapids: Zondervan.

Jossey-Bass also publishes its books in a variety of electronic formats. Some content that appears in print may not be available in electronic books.

Library of Congress Cataloging-in-Publication Data

Halter, Hugh, date
  The tangible kingdom : creating incarnational community : the posture and practices of ancient church now / Hugh Halter and Matt Smay ; foreword by Reggie McNeal. — 1st ed.
      p. cm.
  Includes bibliographical references and index.
  ISBN 978-0-470-18897-2 (cloth)
   1. Communities—Religious aspects—Christianity. 2. Church renewal—United States. 3. Church membership—United States. I. Smay, Matt, 1972– II. Title.
  BV625.H35 2008
  250—dc22
                                                                    2007050264

Printed in the United States of America
FIRST EDITION
HB Printing   10 9 8 7 6 5 4 3 2 1

LEADERSHIP NETWORK TITLES

The Blogging Church: Sharing the Story of Your Church Through Blogs, by Brian Bailey and Terry Storch

Leading from the Second Chair: Serving Your Church, Fulfilling Your Role, and Realizing Your Dreams, by Mike Bonem and Roger Patterson

The Way of Jesus: A Journey of Freedom for Pilgrims and Wanderers, by Jonathan S. Campbell with Jennifer Campbell

Leading the Team-Based Church: How Pastors and Church Staffs Can Grow Together into a Powerful Fellowship of Leaders, by George Cladis

Organic Church: Growing Faith Where Life Happens, by Neil Cole

Off-Road Disciplines: Spiritual Adventures of Missional Leaders, by Earl Creps

Reverse Mentoring: How Young Leaders Can Transform the Church and Why We Should Let Them, Earl Creps

Building a Healthy Multi-Ethnic Church: Mandate, Commitments, and Practices of a Diverse Congregation, by Mark DeYmaz

Leading Congregational Change Workbook, by James H. Furr, Mike Bonem, and Jim Herrington

The Tangible Kingdom: Creating Incarnational Community, by Hugh Halter and Matt Smay

Leading Congregational Change: A Practical Guide for the Transformational Journey, by Jim Herrington, Mike Bonem, and James H. Furr

The Leader's Journey: Accepting the Call to Personal and Congregational Transformation, by Jim Herrington, Robert Creech, and Trisha Taylor

Culture Shift: Transforming Your Church from the Inside Out, by Robert Lewis and Wayne Cordeiro, with Warren Bird

Church Unique: How Missional Leaders Cast Vision, Capture Culture, and Create Movement, by Will Mancini

A New Kind of Christian: A Tale of Two Friends on a Spiritual Journey, by Brian D. McLaren

The Story We Find Ourselves In: Further Adventures of a New Kind of Christian, by Brian D. McLaren

Practicing Greatness: 7 Disciplines of Extraordinary Spiritual Leaders, by Reggie McNeal

The Present Future: Six Tough Questions for the Church, by Reggie McNeal

A Work of Heart: Understanding How God Shapes Spiritual Leaders, by Reggie McNeal

The Millennium Matrix: Reclaiming the Past, Reframing the Future of the Church, by M. Rex Miller

Shaped by God's Heart: The Passion and Practices of Missional Churches, by Milfred Minatrea

The Missional Leader: Equipping Your Church to Reach a Changing World, by Alan J. Roxburgh and Fred Romanuk

The Ascent of a Leader: How Ordinary Relationships Develop Extraordinary Character and Influence, by Bill Thrall, Bruce McNicol, and Ken McElrath

Beyond Megachurch Myths: What We Can Learn from America's Largest Churches, by Scott Thumma and Dave Travis

The Elephant in the Boardroom: Speaking the Unspoken About Pastoral Transitions, by Carolyn Weese and J. Russell Crabtree

CONTENTS

About Leadership Network   xi
Foreword by *Reggie McNeal*   xiii
Acknowledgments   xv
An Invitation . . .   xvii

1. Fiona   1
2. Elvis Has Left the Building   9
3. Tremors   15
4. U-Haul   23
5. Moving Violations   29
6. Posture   37
7. The 1,700-Year Wedgie   49
8. Paradigm   59
9. Jipped   83
10. Another Angle   93
11. Lift Up the Hood   101
12. Tip It Over   107
13. The Hello Experiment   123
14. Leaving   127
15. Listening   131
16. Living Among   135
17. Loving Without Strings   141
18. Inviting In   147
19. Togetherness   157
20. Oneness   163
21. Otherness   171

A Day in the Life . . .   177
Notes   181
The Authors   185
The Missional Church Apprenticeship Practicum   187
Church Resource Ministries   189
Index   191

To our wives, Cheryl and Maren, for living on faith and fumes. You've never complained about the cost of this life, you've shared in every part, and now we hope we make a few dollars on this book so we can take you out for a really nice dinner! To our children, Ryan, Alli, Mckenna, and Maegan. There's not a story here that you weren't a part of. Thanks for letting your dads work in their office.

ABOUT LEADERSHIP NETWORK

Since 1984, Leadership Network has fostered church innovation and growth by diligently pursuing its far-reaching mission statement: to identify, connect, and help high-capacity Christian leaders multiply their impact.

Although Leadership Network's techniques adapt and change as the church faces new opportunities and challenges, the organization's work follows a consistent and proven pattern: Leadership Network brings together entrepreneurial leaders who are focused on similar ministry initiatives. The ensuing collaboration—often across denominational lines—creates a strong base from which individual leaders can better analyze and refine their own strategies. Peer-to-peer interaction, dialogue, and sharing inevitably accelerate participants' innovation and ideas. Leadership Network further enhances this process through developing and distributing highly targeted ministry tools and resources, including audio and video programs, special reports, e-publications, and online downloads.

With Leadership Network's assistance, today's Christian leaders are energized, equipped, inspired, and better able to multiply their own dynamic Kingdom-building initiatives.

Launched in 1996 in conjunction with Jossey-Bass (a Wiley imprint), Leadership Network Publications present thoroughly researched and innovative concepts from leading thinkers, practitioners, and pioneering churches. The series collectively draws from a range of disciplines, with individual titles offering perspective on one or more of five primary areas:

1. Enabling effective leadership
2. Encouraging life-changing service
3. Building authentic community
4. Creating Kingdom-centered impact
5. Engaging cultural and demographic realities

For additional information on the mission or activities of Leadership Network, please contact:

Leadership Network
(800) 765-5323
client.care@leadnet.org

FOREWORD

Reggie McNeal

RECENTLY I WALKED BY a "church" that was holding "services" on a Sunday morning in an upscale community in Northern California. Organ music drifted out of the open doors, spilling onto the streets where passersby made their way to coffee shops, art galleries, and antique stores, oblivious to the goings-on of the band of worshipers ensconced behind stucco walls.

Is this situation worrisome to that congregation? Apparently not. No one was outside to engage anyone on the street. Nametags were on prominent display in the entry plaza next to the "sanctuary." The clear message was "Members only." If you wandered in on the activities absent a nametag, you'd stick out like a sore thumb.

Contrast this picture with what you see and experience as you read about the early days of the Christian movement in the Book of Acts. The Kingdom was spreading like a virus, invading every aspect of society. There wasn't a possibility of containing it inside a building; it was unleashed onto the street.

If you are a church leader, you will self-select into your own future of spiritual expression. Either you will participate in some kind of religious activity that is increasingly disconnected from its surrounding culture, or you will join the ranks of those who want to experience the life of a Jesus follower. You don't need much help in making the first choice. However, if you want to participate in the Kingdom here and now, you might need some help in knowing how to prepare for that. Enter Hugh Halter and Matt Smay.

I met Hugh and Matt at a Christian leaders' gathering. As I got to know them, I sensed transparency, authenticity, an inquisitive spirit, humility, and . . . joy! As these two guys shared the story of Adullam, their community in the Denver area, I kept thinking, "This story needs to be told." Months later, I was thrilled to find out it was happening. Now you have their journey notes in your hand.

I can recommend this book for lots of reasons. It will help you re-language your conversations as a Christian leader so that you can imagine different solutions for greater missional effectiveness. Their cultural analysis is good missiology. The descriptions they provide of how they operate give you concrete ways to move forward if you want to become more incarnational. This book could change your mind about how you view church, mission, and the culture we've been called to influence. Its strength is that it pops open new thought while telling about how the ideas flesh out in real life.

But what Hugh and Matt most want to do is give you hope. Hope of experiencing the Kingdom here and now. They certainly helped me believe all over again. Now you can, too.

ACKNOWLEDGMENTS

AS WE'VE TRAVERSED THROUGH our story, many people have had a genuine influence, and we're honored to recognize them here.

To our CRM family, led by Sam Metcalf and Paul Rhoads: Thanks for living out your motto of "empowering leaders worldwide." As well to our CRM personal support teams, who have sacrificially given to this work, thus giving us a chance to be missionaries in our own country.

To Steve Ogne, Bill Malick, and Bob Logan, for helping architect the tools that set in motion a church-planting movement.

To our Aussie mates, Alan Hirsch and Mike Frost, along with the FORGE Mission Training Network, for adding your fresh voice to our Western context.

To our Adullam family: Our story is your story, and we look forward to our common call in Denver.

To Grace Chapel in Denver, Imago Dei Community and Open Bible Church in Portland, and Core Community in Omaha: Thanks for making small but critical investments in our story and looking beyond your own church walls.

To Phil and Laina Graf, for your formative work with us, for living out this book more than any other people we've met, and for the free Harley.

To our literary agent Greg Johnson, and editor extraordinaire Becky Johnson: You know how much you did!

AN INVITATION . . .

IF YOU'RE THE TYPE of reader who likes to skip introductions, now's your chance. No one's watching, so if you'd prefer to get to the action and angst, you'll be satisfied as our story and chapters unfold. But if you can hold tight with us for a few pages, the things we say here can truly help set up the book.

Picture, if you will . . .

A small boat drifts calmly along the southeast coastline of Italy. The weary sailor steering the boat wakens from a short sleep after a hard night fighting the currents, wind, and rain. He's come from across the seas in search of a quaint fishing village known for its hospitable inhabitants, constant sunshine, cool breezes, and hope of a new future. He's fled from the opposite—a place of corruption, greed, tension, violence, and despair. He had heard about this peaceful enclave from others who sent back word of the possibilities available to anyone who wishes to come. But the word also came with a caution. They said this harbor town, surrounded by steep jagged cliffs, is not easy to get to. It used to be easy to access, but the unseen reefs and rocks have shipwrecked so many that now the downed vessels themselves have become hindrances for others who try to get in. The carnage is visible to everyone. And most people, like this traveler, though drawn powerfully to what they have been told is on shore, are reluctant to navigate the wreckage.

Of course, some people can find their way in. A way has always been open to those who listened carefully to the local guides. Years ago, they erected three buoys out in the middle of the harbor. They stood 20 feet high off the surface of the water and were placed a quarter-mile apart starting from the neck of the bay, through the obstacles, and into the docks.

Because the guides had to be built upon dangerous underwater reefs, the locals knew not to steer directly for the pylons but instead to use them as guides for a correct angle of entry. The problem was that this was counterintuitive for most of the savvy, well-sailed skippers who preferred to rely on their experience or their trusty vessels than on the wisdom of those who knew what was under the surface.

So what is this tale of a perilous harbor and difficult navigation doing in a book about Christianity and the church? The answer is that it represents both the hope and the despair so many are feeling and experiencing in the idea of "church." For years, we've hung on to the hope that God loves the world and intends to bring his redemptive ways to a broken human condition through his people, his church. We read epic accounts in our holy scriptures about people who changed humanity and experienced a level of communal power that we long to find. We've preached and listened to preachers who tell a story we'd all love to find ourselves in, yet we feel the gap between what we hear and talk about and what we experience.

For far too many of us, when we hear the word *church*, our eyes tear up, turn bloodshot, or glaze over, with emotions that represent the irrelevance of our communal expressions, or because we don't know what to think anymore. Our faith and loyalty used to keep us on board, but now reality is beginning to curl over both like a 20-foot wave.

The idea of God's Kingdom is now relegated to the realm of heaven, the afterlife, and we just assume that we won't get to see God and his beautiful redemptive plan until we pass over. The church therefore becomes something we may not need anymore, something that at best is worth only our recreational enjoyment. Our massive hope about God, his Kingdom, and our place in a unique community of people who change the world is all but dead, and we're left feeling like the searcher who wants in but is reluctant to face the dangers of navigating our collective faith and purpose.

If you're like the authors of this book, you've gone down with a ship or two trying to make the Kingdom story tangible. You may have tried a few different churches, methods, programs, leaders, teachers, styles, and sizes only to find yourself stuck on a ship that seems to be attracting no one and can barely hold your interest.

Maybe you've abandoned the boat and are treading water, hoping a rescue vessel will appear. Perhaps you've abandoned the vessel and are swimming for your life, trying to get away from the shipwreck of bad (or less than fulfilling) church experiences. Even if another boat appeared, you wouldn't trust it to take you into the harbor—you've wrecked too many times. Or, you're already sitting up on the rocks, sopping wet, staring off into theological oblivion, wondering how much of the ancient story can really be true for today.

Maybe you've captained one of these ships and, without knowing it, found yourself sailing toward irrelevance. You have people on board, but they seem to have lost their heart. You would love to change course. You would be happy to sail toward something new even if uncharted, but you wonder if you'd be sailing alone. Quite possibly you've lost your energy, and even if the wind of a new program came up, you'd be too tired to open the main sail again. Maybe it's just better to drop anchor and wait until the storm blows over?

If you don't identify with any of this story, then this book may be a waste of your time. However, if something seemed to prick in your heart or pique your mind, then maybe our story will be of help to you.

Our Purpose

Our Purpose is simple. We want to talk to you about the church. We want to let you know that the unsettling feelings you are experiencing are ones that hundreds of thousands of people are also working through. We also want to give you hope and a real-life picture of a preferred future.

At the same time, our intent isn't to try to figure everything out for you, because we don't have all the answers. We won't tell you to dry yourself off and get back on another boat. We also won't tell you which boats are good or bad. We don't care if your context is mega-church, house church, or whatever-church. We don't think it matters. Therefore, we won't ask you to swim toward *our* pylons, as if we've got the corner on the *one way* toward safety. What we hope to do is to explain what's below the surface, which way the currents are moving, and what the guideposts or pylons represent. If these thoughts make sense to you, as they have to us, we hope your intangible dream of God and his church—the Kingdom Jesus talked about—will become tangible.

Matt and I wrote this book because so many people pestered us to put our story down on paper. We had spent seven years traveling throughout America and overseas, training church planters, church dreamers, and existing church leaders in the hope that they might become more *missional and incarnational*. These two words together describe an orientation toward the ancient faith communities described in the Book of Acts and throughout history, who lived a countercultural, communal experience that always influenced the cultures they found themselves in. These missional/incarnational communities were therefore the natural framework God's church was and must still be built upon if we are to continue their rich legacy of making apprentices of Jesus worldwide. Although small and unsanctioned, these early communities were powerful and authoritative. Although they were on the run and decentralized, they were organized and strategic. Although they didn't know much about starting or growing churches, they did both naturally. Church just happened, and it was deeply meaningful.

We have found bits and pieces of their story in our story, and we hope this book captures enough of both to help dry you off and begin to navigate your way back toward God's mission in the world.

If you're discouraged with your own spiritual story or with your church's struggle to meaningfully influence and engage those around you, this book may give you hope that it can still be done. If you're discouraged with church altogether, our story may help you reimagine a new community, one that you might even want to start or participate in.

Most of the stories in the book come from Hugh. Matt helps coach you and your community by contributing the Reflections at the end of each chapter.

A word about the tone in which this book is written. As you read, we believe that you'll come to trust that our heart is for the church, both existing and emerging. For our own mental sanity and to help us write, we take pokes, jabs, or make light of how we have done church. Yes, we could have sanitized this a little so as not to offend anyone, but we've concluded it would be unfair to thousands of people who need to hear some emotion that they can identify with. We need to be honest with our story. We know we're not alone in our thoughts and feelings, and we hope that the exercise of listening to each other, laughing at ourselves, dreaming of a preferred future will help pull us together so that we are all pulling in the same direction.

Our Story

Our story is simple: As a bunch of friends living in Denver who were committed to live out ancient ways in a modern context of community, communion, and mission, we suddenly found ourselves in the company of followers, most of whom did not come from a meaningful church background or any church background at all.

Initially, we were resistant to starting another church, since we ourselves were still wet from previous shipwrecks. But something intangible happened that sparked our collective interest. We saw jaded Christians smiling again; we found people consistently initiating spiritual interest in our communities, and we, as leaders, found ourselves overwhelmed with the enjoyment of church while desperately trying not to be a church. When we could no longer deny God's unique work among us, we named our community *Adullam*, an Old Testament cave name that means "refuge." (When we mention "in Adullam," we don't mean—or say—"*at* Adullam." This is intentional, as we don't want to convey that Adullam is a building. You'll see why as the book goes on.)

We're just four years into our adventure as Adullam. We're experiencing some unusual success, but we're not measuring that success by huge leaps in attendance or a shiny new building. Compared to 3 million people in Denver, the number of people in Adullam is silly to mention. We meet in homes, pubs, and rented facilities. Our goal isn't to attract Christian people to our worship service but to be the faithful church in small pockets throughout our city. We are creating places of inclusive belonging where God's alternative Kingdom can be experienced.

What About You?

Even though we believe we've learned some valuable things in Adullam, you'd be wise to proceed with caution in reading our story. We can't give you a formula for how to fix your church, so please don't cling to our pylons. We haven't cured the cancer of spiritual consumerism, but what we *do* have are some intentional practices and habits of life that will help you and your faith community make God's Kingdom more tangible.

What you find in this book may go against the grain of your life and past church experience. You won't find methods or mission statements. We don't think people are drawn to methods or statements. But, you *will* find some practical habits we can coach you to engage.

If you are a church leader, pastor, or church planter, this book will give you hope that ancient, incarnational ways of church make more sense in the long run than spinning all the plates for spiritual consumers or fighting the uphill battle of trying to attract people to your church. You'll also discover that sending your people out is safer than trying to keep them happy inside the programs, small groups, and four walls of the building. We believe that as a leader, you'll have more fun modeling a new way of life than running programs or preaching to the choir.

If you are a concerned non-paid saint, and you are reading this book, you may find that it helps you vent frustrations, rethink important theology, and offers practical ways of readjusting your life around God's mission in the world. You'll see why you are in as good—or better—a position than your pastor to bring the gospel into the lives of those you love, no matter where you live.

The denominational leader or those in positions of influence and resourcing may find that this book helps you make necessary changes to your church before the sun sets on the institutionalized form of Christianity you may be trying to maintain (with little success). We hope it will also give you some ideas of how to use your influence, resources, and networks to launch new incarnational "Christ going into the world" forms of ministry.

Finally, maybe you're not even a follower of Christ, or you're unsure about who he really is, or what a Christian is. If you're reading this, maybe a Christian friend gave you this book because he is not sure how to help you get past the confines and contraptions of the institutional church and get at what it's really all about. She may also be rethinking everything and truly value your friendship during her process of spiritual renovation.

If you stick with us to the end, our hope is that you can forgive your past or present experiences with the myopic forms of Christianity and help us create new places of belonging, benevolence, and blessing around the world.

At the end of each chapter, we provide Reflection questions for contemplation or discussion. We recommend that, if possible, you read through this book with a group of people—perhaps a mix of Christian folk (jaded, spiritually disoriented, but open). The process probably won't work well (or maybe at all) with Christians who tend to know too much, talk too much, and judge too much.

A note on the harbor illustration. It may seem to go against the idea of this book. As you read through the chapters, you'll likely get a strong sense that we're calling the church out from its safe environment. You might expect, therefore, that we'd ask you to leave your safe harbor and sail off into the stormy seas. But the harbor doesn't represent safety. It represents God's Kingdom. His life. His reality. What we believe we should find and what church should direct us to. In actuality, it communicates exactly what we believe is the call of the church: Find and help others find God's beautiful city.

Again, so as not to confuse you on the "voice" of the book, we point out that most of the stories come from Hugh. Matt helps coach you and your community through the reflection time at the end of each chapter.

○
_____

Reflection

As you ponder the metaphor of this sailor, this village, the wreckage, and the people, reflect on your own experience with church. What aspects have been meaningful, and which experiences do you hope to put behind you?

_____
○

THE TANGIBLE KINGDOM

FIONA

MY WIFE, CHERYL, ONCE SAID, "If God had not called Hugh to plant churches, he'd never go to church." As a church consultant and a missionary with an organization that is totally committed to missional leadership for the church (culturally savvy, deep in character, clear in calling, and committed to incarnational ways of life and church), I have lived most of my adult years in great tension. If there's one thing I've learned as a trainer and consultant, no one trusts you unless you share your wounds, so I think it's right that I talk a little about mine. I hope that as you begin to understand my saga, you will sense God's invitation to trust him wherever he may take you.

Since I mentioned in the "Invitation" that I enjoy starting new churches, you may have some perspective on my initial misery: No money, no external respect, very little denominational support, and the personal conflict of never finding much meaning in church. I didn't like to sing, I didn't feel I could integrate my non-Christian friends into the Sunday experience, and it seemed to take up time that I thought would be better spent with "normal" folks. Add to that, a deathly fear of public speaking and my propensity for introversion, what you get is a tough week . . . over and over again.

So why do I plant churches? Why do I train other church planters? Why not be a lumberjack or park ranger and hide out in the seclusion of a deep, dark forest? There are several reasons.

First, I believe in the church. I believe God loves his church, and that he's quite ticked that his bride looks like "Fiona the ogre" instead of Cameron Diaz. I believe he desires a beautiful bride—one the world looks to with awe and amazement, with intrigue and longing.

Second, and more personal, I believe that God, with his unique sense of humor, designed me with evangelistic antennae. They've been there since I was in the eighth grade. I've always wondered about people who didn't know Christ. For the most part, I've tended to feel much more drawn to them than to my Christian brothers and sisters. Those outside the faith have been my best friends. I worship to the tune of U2, Switchfoot, and Peter Gabriel instead of KLUV; I often find myself inspired by the selfless compassion non-Christians have for the world without knowing the Creator of it; I'm regularly amazed at the way so many "pagans" accept all people and, quite frankly, seem to be a lot more fun to hang out with. As I've talked hundreds of times with a veritable plethora of "Sojourners" (spiritually disoriented God seekers) about their views of Christianity, God, the Bible, the church, I have to admit: I not only understand why they aren't attracted to any of it, but I've also become a bit repulsed by certain strains of our evangelical tribe. Sure, I see these Sojourners' ignorance and selfishness, their vice and frailty, but it doesn't seem any worse by degree than what I see in my own life or the lives of those I've rubbed shoulders with in the pews, throughout the past couple of decades.

In some ways, I think I've always wanted more for Sojourners than what I had personally experienced in church. I guess I always wanted more for myself, as well.

When I walk into Starbucks, I don't think about coffee. That's predetermined . . . tall black Americano. I ponder the lives of everyone I see. I wonder about their spiritual journeys, their highs and lows . . . and where they look for direction in their search. My initial assumption is that in any room full of people, very few know Christ. I ask myself how I could get into their lives or how a conversation might begin. I don't see them as projects—that wouldn't go very far. I see them as souls the Lord loves who simply haven't seen or heard an accurate message about the Kingdom. I always feel confident that I may one day be talking with them about life and God. Oddly enough, this seems to happen all the time.

I've accepted that God has gifted me this way, and I don't expect that everyone will understand or feel the depth of my passion for the spiritually disoriented, nor that my habits of life and engagement will fit everyone. However, I do believe that since you're reading this, you may share something I rarely say out loud: I can't picture any of these people, or my friends, or your friends, going to church . . . any church . . . *ever!*

It was just after I resigned from our first church plant five years ago that this doubt about church reached a high point. We had pioneered a good little community out of the metro corridor in Portland, Oregon. It was our vision to help a diverse group of people come together in worship and mission to the city. To model our seriousness regarding multiethnic issues, we merged our predominantly white congregation with an African American congregation. Because of our missional bent and focus on those outside our church, this community did well and became quite effective in helping people who had not been among our ranks find a home with us. All went well, especially for those outside the church who found in us a reflection of what they had hoped church could be. It grew, and we sensed great favor with God, the city, and the people.

We thought we had thoroughly prepared our leaders for the inevitable problems; and yet, tragically, underneath the surface of this beautiful church—in spite of our best efforts—an invisible tension evolved within the leadership. Issues began to arise over who should preach and how we should preach; whether or not the ushers should be allowed to wear white gloves; how to integrate the traditional black choir with the untraditional worship team; how to break up the salaries based on the perception of who's in charge; whether or not we should continue the tradition of "pastor appreciation week"; and other assorted "how to do church" issues.

Despite all the prayer, fasting, and even the attempt to bring in outside consultants to help us work through these issues, eventually insecurity, tradition, pride, churchiness, and fear not only crept in but stood up and loudly declared they were going to have their way. It was like watching the weather channel describe a hurricane that's coming directly at your city, and you can't do anything to stop it.

In the end, my worst fears were realized: This match that we had thought was made in heaven would break up due to irreconcilable differences. My previous memory of another good church gone bad was watching my cell phone fly over our kid's swing set and a 20-foot rhododendron tree, finally smashing into a hundred pieces . . . this after my last conversation with the remaining leader of said church. Plastic, metal, and all my phone numbers (including my ESPN satellite link) smashed and scattered, just like my vision, my friends, and my hopes of a perfect church.

Cheryl, my wife, who always seems to catch me in these situations, whispered through the screen window, "Nice throw. Now what are you going to do?"

The next week we stood up and blessed the congregation, resigned, and exiled ourselves to a town two hours south in hope that the church would survive. I wish I could tell you that God taught me something, or that there was a deep biblical lesson in all this, or that the church eventually rousted itself and did great, but I can't. People were hurt—badly. I cried more than I ever cried before. I doubted God internally and verbally as I vented my frustrations. In the end, I realized the problem with church is simply church and Christians (present company included), our usual failings as human beings, and a lot of evangelical dogma we have blindly believed in, and accommodated by our behavior, for many years.

It was at this point that I became a card-carrying member of what I call the "jaded" denomination. You know, people who have a hard time finding coherence between their faith in God and their experience in the church; people who are sick of that same old song, same lingo, same methods, same discouraging results, and same spiritual emptiness. No, I didn't leave the church entirely, like 25-million-plus-and-growing, other dechurched Christians are doing in America. But I wanted to.

My dream church became my nightmare church. The resulting tension became so bad that I decided the only way to avoid reliving another similar experience but still retain my ministerial credentials was to become a church consultant. In Greek, church consultant—*Ecclesia Consultia*—means "one who has paid his dues and has the scars to prove it."

After we resigned from the church, God threw us a life preserver by linking us with Church Resource Ministries, a unique mission's organization that was committed to training missional leaders for the church. In the interim, I agreed to help a friend by taking an associate pastor role in his congregation. I saw this as a way to get out of Portland and dull the throbbing memories of my most recent church implosion as well as get set up for this new season of consulting.

Besides all the agony related to ministry, we were dealing with my son's health problems. Ryan has had severe epilepsy from birth. He has a handful of grand mal seizures a day, every day. His fight for life and quality of life has made this journey harder than skateboarding uphill on a gravel road, but somehow we seemed to keep the wheels rolling. Now, however, I figured it would be a great time to use this situation as the final justification to tap out, call for a sub, adopt the loser limp, and justify coming off the field. I handed the missional ball back to God and took what I felt was a much deserved breather.

We packed our bags quickly and drove two hours south to Eugene, Oregon, to work alongside our dear pastor friend and a beautiful church plant that had grown to about a thousand people. My job description was to "just be there." No kidding! No specific tasks, no specific goals, just provide support for my friend and anyone who needed some nonspecific help. *Perfect*, I thought. I get to enjoy hanging out with my buddy, help him out a little, and have the bonus of playing golf with him. I won't have to carry any major burdens, I won't have any pressure, very little speaking to do, no one knows me in this town, and I have a consistent paycheck! Sweet!

This delightful new season began beautifully. I would hop on my bike every morning and ride along a lovely river to the church, check in with dear Julia, the secretary, and then do whatever I could to help out. Then it was back on the bike to home. On my way back, I'd often pull my Cabella five-piece fly rod out of my backpack and try to land a nice rainbow out of the McKenzie or Willamette river. Never caught one, but I sure enjoyed living the dream. Once home, I could shut off my mind and open my heart and focus on my family. Even my closest friends thought the break was good for me.

About three months into my nonspecific utopia, Cheryl and I were having coffee, and as she stirred some vanilla creamer into her coffee, she made this observation: "You're not going to make it."

"What are you talking about?" I replied, taking another swig of java.

"Just doing the church thing."

"No, we'll make it. The stability is great, we're paying the bills, we have a beautiful home with a five-spout jetted bathtub, a microwave that knows exactly how long to pop popcorn, and I'm hardly ever stressed. . . . You better believe we'll make it."

You can assume the rest: Wives are always right.

That same week, I was booked to do a church plant training seminar in New York City. It was just five weeks after September 11, 2001, and we were one of the first airplanes to land when LaGuardia Airport reopened. Each evening after the training sessions, we headed out to grab dinner and ended up frequenting an Irish pub in Queens. Unlike LA or Nashville, where an Irish pub can be run by either Englishmen or Koreans, in New York, the staff are from Ireland. They are my people (Irish red-haired toughs who enjoy a good fight). Over several nights we got to know a few of the waitresses and some of their stories about growing up in Ireland.

One young waitress, Fiona, shared about her religious upbringing in Northern Ireland. As you can imagine, she seemed to have some faith in God, but she wasn't too fond of Protestants, Catholics, or the church. After our training event was over, all my fellow staff flew back home, but I had one more night to stay in NYC. About midnight I decided to go back to the pub for one final pint and a chance to say good-bye to my new friends.

The Yankees were in the playoffs, and the place was packed. I walked in and headed toward the bar looking for a seat. As I made my way deeper into the crowd, I heard Fiona calling two bartenders over to meet me.

"This is the guy I was telling you about," she said. "You've got to hear how he talks about God."

Suffice it to say, you don't get that type of enthusiasm from most church members. At that introduction, the room split to make room for me, a scene not unlike when Wyatt Earp and Doc Holiday enter a mangy tavern in the movie *Tombstone*.

Over the course of the next few hours, I got to share a bit of my story and listen to theirs. As the bar thinned out, the bartenders invited me to help them clean up. Eventually, everyone was gone except Fiona, a few other waitresses, bartenders, and the owner. We all sat around one table as they asked one question after another. Their questions were so sincere, their anger so justified. Yes, they were jaded, too, but their intrigue with me seemed honest and open. I knew I couldn't talk about church. I knew I couldn't share the four spiritual laws or tell them I was a pastor. I just talked about the only thing I knew they might like: Jesus and the alternative world he called the "Kingdom of God." They loved it just as much as I did, and lapped it up like hungry pups. When it was time to part, they all hugged me and let me pray for them, and then I left.

It was just before 6:00 a.m. as I opened the heavy pub door to head back to my hotel. The sun was just starting to creep out above the buildings.

As soon as the door slammed behind me, I met God again.

In the same way that Aslan breathed on the frozen characters in Narnia, melting them back to life, so my heart that had been on hold started to thaw and ache again. I began to cry. Harder than I've ever cried. Heaving tears, shaking uncontrollably. I had to sit down on the dirty curb and put my hands over my head so no one would see me. I'm sure I looked like a drunk puking in the street. I suddenly knew what God was doing. I knew he was saying I could trust him again with my son's health, that I could trust him with our finances again, that he'd just been in that pub with me, and therefore, there was no better place for me to be.

The call was clear.

The Twin Towers had just gone down; the world seemed fragile at best. Golf, fishing, the comfort of my custom home, perfectly popped popcorn, and shifting the burden of people onto someone else seemed like luxuries I would gladly give up for this feeling of being fully alive and fully engaged.

The call was to get back in the game. To enter the tension again!

The voice was about his church again.

The challenge was to stop being jaded long enough to crack the wardrobe open to view God's Kingdom again, God's story again, God's mission again.

I know there are millions of the jaded here in the States, likely millions more throughout the world. I empathize. But the truth is, we all have to get beyond our cynicism so we don't end up watching *Oprah* or *Larry King* for spiritual guidance. (That's a joke, but there is some sad reality to it.)

On the way home I called Cheryl. I tried to soften the edges of my experience, but I muttered out something about how "God was messing with me again." She seemed prepared and even whimsical in her acceptance of another challenge. Once home, I was able to share the details, and then I asked her what city she'd like to go to. In less than thirty minutes, she picked Denver. I wish I could say it was a divine leading, a result of hours of prayer and fasting. But it wasn't. She picked the Mile High City because she loved John Elway. Not exactly the Star of Bethlehem, but I took it as a sign from God anyway. Just ten months after we'd left our hometown of Portland to lie low in Eugene, we painfully resigned from my friend's church, packed up the U-Haul and headed to the Rockies, still somewhat jaded but willing to let God revive my hopes again—a vision for the greater church and maybe another small church that someday could be an easy and relaxed home for searching souls like Fiona and her friends . . . and myself.

o

Reflection

o Describe some times in your life when you've wanted to tap out on God and the activities of the church.

o Describe the last time your heart broke for someone.

o

2

ELVIS HAS LEFT THE BUILDING

PUSHING OPEN THE RUSTIC wood doors of that Irish pub signaled a new search for me. It meant embracing faith again; it meant acknowledging my own failures and spiritual lethargy; it meant that I would have to allow the pain of a broken world and the call of Christ to once again dictate my future; and it meant rethinking . . . really thinking through God's idea of the church and his Kingdom.

This book is about creating something new and different from the institutions and structures of church that have caused millions of Christians to leave the organized forms during the past twenty years—the forms that are causing so many God seekers to look everywhere except the church on the corner for spiritual help or meaning for life. According to the Barna Group, "Only 3 out of 10 twentysomethings (31 percent) attend church in a typical week, compared to 4 out of 10 of those in their 30s (42 percent) and nearly half of all adults age 40 and older (49 percent)."[1]

Although we call for church to change, we do not suggest that we obliterate all the forms and habits of Christianity. Change must be about *new*, which to us means "fresh, bright, something that intuitively feels right, that causes us not only to dream but to move on our dreams." That kind of new is good if it compels us into a world of faith again where we can battle fear and despondency with action that makes a difference. That kind of new is okay, but it really isn't new. It's just been hidden, or covered, or we've been distracted from it. Quite possibly, you may never have seen or experienced it, so you don't know what it would look like even if it showed up.

This type of new is about a returning. Returning to something ancient, something tried, something true and trustworthy. Something that has rerouted the legacies of families, nations, kings, and peasants. Something that has caused hundreds of thousands to give up security, reputation, and their lives. What we're returning to has always been and must still be revolutionary. What we need to dig up, recover, and find again is the life of the Kingdom and Jesus' community . . . the church. As we do, we'll find that it's not American . . . it's "other world"; it's not evangelicalism, it's much more holistic and integrated into real life. It's not anti-church; it's pro-church. It's about the type of church that Jesus would go to, the type he died to give flight to. It's not about success, size of buildings, budget, or "salvations." It is about being faithful to live Christ's alternative ways in the world again.

Even now, as I'm sitting at a Starbucks in the final week of editing this book, I just took a break to talk to a guy named Don. Don grew up in a non-practicing Catholic home, watched his father convert to a Seventh-Day Adventist tradition, but only remembers the types of meat he couldn't eat. His wife hates the idea of God, and Don's already expressed his love of God but his disdain for organized church. Since he seemed open to talk, I lobbed up this question: "If Christianity was only about finding a group of people to live life with, who shared openly their search for God and allowed anyone, regardless of behavior, to seek too, and who collectively lived by faith to make the world a little more like Heaven, would you be interested?"

"Hell yes!" was his reply. He continued. "Are there churches like that?"

What Don is asking for is the Kingdom of God made tangible. His twenty-year-old daughter just a had a child out of wedlock; his wife won't speak to him or help discipline his other teenage daughter, who is bankrupting them with credit card purchases. He's done with religion, he's done with church, but I can't get him to shut up so I can finish editing the book because he is desperate for tangible help. I'm going to take a break from this and pray with him before he moves on.

Where We Are

To get from where we are today to this ancient-now Tangible Kingdom, let's start by taking a sip of old stale wine—a hard look at where we are now. What we have collectively invested in without seeing much return. What has kept us busy without giving us very good results at what Jesus asked us to accomplish: the proliferation of global blessing and the making of apprentices of Jesus. People that look, act, and sound like he did!

Yes, we have big churches, churches that grow and do much good in the world, but let's be honest: Do people take us Christians seriously? Do they respect us and our way of life? Do the spiritually hungry look to the average evangelical church for help, or would they rather go buy a self-help book at Barnes & Noble?

How long has it been since you knew someone who came to faith for the first time? I'm not talking about in a youth group setting or in children's church. I'm talking about an adult who had no idea about God but who has since found faith in Christ and rearranged his or her entire life around his? We've been working with pastors of mega-churches, house churches, and many new churches, and the reality of "nonconversions" is staggering.

We have churches everywhere, but they smell musty, fussy, clubby, judgmental, mean, punishing, ungenerous, and are not compelling people to come or stay. Almost every statistical reference to the church indicates that we not only can't draw people, but we can't even keep the ones we have. That's right, Elvis has left the building! Statistics, of course, aren't everything. And you can sometimes make them say anything you want. A few hard numbers by way of illustration might put this in perspective:

o "The Barna Group reveals that one-third of the adult population (34 percent) has not attended any type of church service or activity, other than a special event such as a funeral or wedding, during the past six months. Citing past research that discovered most unchurched adults were formerly churched, the new study indicates that six out of ten unchurched people (62 percent) consider themselves to be Christian, four percent say they are Jewish, four percent are associated with an Eastern religion, and 24 percent say they are atheist."[2]

o The most recent research studies by the Barna Group "reveals that one out of every three adults (33 percent) is classified as unchurched—meaning they have not attended a religious service of any type during the past six months. When these statistics are projected across the aggregate adult population, the numbers are staggering. An estimated 73 million adults are presently unchurched. When teens and children are added, the total swells to roughly 100 million Americans."[3]

○ "Since 1991, the adult population in the United States has grown by 15 percent. During that same period the number of adults who do not attend church has nearly doubled, rising from 39 million to 75 million—a 92 percent increase."[4]

○ "Roughly half of all churches in America did not add one new person through conversion growth last year."[5]

○ "In America, it takes the combined effort of eighty-five Christians working over an entire year to produce one convert."[6]

Thus, say Tom Clegg and Warren Bird, "The inescapable conclusion is that we must throw out any notion that God is truly at the center of the church's heart in North America. The shift in society's view of the church has resulted in the marginalization of the church and the secularization of society. Christianity has lost its place at the center of American life. Christians must learn how to live the gospel as a distinct people who no longer occupy the center of society. We must learn to build relational bridges that win a hearing."[7]

Without blaming church leaders, the church at large, or denominations, we can at least acknowledge that something must change to reverse the trends. We need to start by doing some things we *haven't* been doing, and we must stop doing some things that we *have* been doing. The world around us is growing increasingly disinterested in our Christian story. They respect us less and less every year, and our own people are jumping off the ship just to save their faith. Worse, our children, for the first time in American history, aren't following us in faith. According to the Baylor Religion Survey, "Persons aged 18 to 30 are three times more likely to have no religious affiliation (18.6 percent) than are persons aged 65 or older (5.4 percent)."[8]

Please hear us. We're not here to deconstruct, to point fingers, to make fun of, or to name names. We gently want to acknowledge, like an alcoholic in front of his AA friends, that the wineskin has cracked, that we have a serious problem.

Let's all say it together, "Hi, my name is [fill in the blank] and I'm a part of a national Christian movement that doesn't taste good anymore."

If you're in a church that is growing and people are enthusiastic, you should count yourself lucky. But if you evaluated your statistics objectively, you'd likely come to the conclusion that most of the growth of your church is transfer growth, with new people coming from another church.

Is it wrong or less spiritual to meet the needs of Christians who perhaps aren't growing at other churches, who can move to the next level with Christ under the shepherding of a different church? Sure, this is important. If this is the goal of your church, fine. But be careful about calling this "growth." Churches can make a difference in some way with some Christians, but it's unlikely they're making a dent in culture by reaching the unreached or helping the truly disenfranchised.

Obviously, helping disenfranchised Christians find hope again in church is a good thing. We are not against "transfer" growth, but we have to call it what it is.

I bring this up to illustrate how many Christians or God fearers there are outside of church now. The death of so many churches is creating a feeder system for what some may call *relevant* or *visionary* or *emergent* churches. It is good that we're "rechurching" America, but we also need to realize that when the feeder churches finally die off, everyone will feel the paucity of churchgoers. If we don't focus on the "brand spanking new" conversion of people, neighborhoods, and cities, in just a few short years, we'll be going to refurbished church buildings to have a pint of Guinness and play blackjack, bingo, or bridge with the neighbors. If Adullam ends up like a normal American church, I'll be the one at the bar pouring a beer for myself.

It's time to take a serious pause and reflect on the church as it has been in the past and is presently. Although we are wholeheartedly calling for a new church to emerge, we need to be careful with what we mean by *emerging*. When people are talking about emerging church, they're not talking about brand new ways of doing wild and crazy forms of church. Emerging doesn't have to be about lighting candles, finger painting during worship, offering tattooing in the church foyer, or reducing deep theological truths down to the level of a comic book. It doesn't mean church for young people only.

Have you considered that when the unchurched baby boomers reach retirement age, they'll represent one of our most unreached people groups? Let's coin a phrase: "GenG" (Geriatric Generation). Therefore, if we're committed to reaching one of the fastest growing segments, "emerging church" may be based in retirement centers and have as its primary cultural engagement reruns of *Happy Days, Leave It to Beaver*, and free denture giveaways.

Certainly, in the real sense, the church has been around for quite some time and might take offense at being considered "nonemerged." In another sense, the church is always emerging. Therefore, the issue has nothing to do with "emerging," but *what* is emerging and *if* the new forms of Christianity and church are authentic to the original ideals of Christ and appropriate to the culture that has lost interest in organized Christendom.

The lack of "conversions" are not the real problem. That's just a visible symptom of the level of blindness in our present forms of church and the fact that our Christian kingdoms need more of God's Kingdom to "emerge" within us.

Now if you didn't need to read all the stats, or hear the bad news, take the time you just saved and go drop off a nice bottle of wine to your neighbor with a note saying, "Love to get to know you guys sometime. Call and we'll enjoy this bottle together."

When you come back, let's get to the real issue: tension.

○

Reflection

○ Thinking about what you just read, and considering what Jesus said in Matthew 5:13—"You are the salt of the earth. But if the salt loses its saltiness how can it be made salty again? It is no longer good for anything, except to be thrown out and trampled by men"—what are some of the ways you believe we're losing our saltiness?

○ What do you think the increasing disinterest of the culture toward church means for the future of the church?

○

3

TREMORS

NOT LONG AGO MATT AND I were in Australia. The last night before we returned home, Matt woke me up in the middle of the night and said, "I'm not feeling too well."

For some people this would be no big deal, but after spending nearly every day with Matt the past five years, I've learned that he could have a 10-inch spike sticking out his head and not complain. I tried to help him describe how he was feeling, but he struggled. "I feel like I'm shaking from the inside out," was all he could say.

Over the next few minutes, I checked his pulse, questioned him on what he ate, and did a general "clueless friend" medical exam. We still had no idea what could be wrong. Minute by minute, however, he seemed to be more uncomfortable, and his shaking became so bad we had to hold him down.

We then intuitively did what you do when someone is almost levitating off the bed. We prayed. When it was over, we wondered if what we had been doing in Melbourne could have seriously ticked off someone in the underworld. The strangest thing was how clear Matt could have been in his mind while his body was out of control. He had incredible tremors and tension in his face but no idea why.

I share this story (which I finish later in the chapter) as an illustration of what Matt and I have seen all over the country and world as we hear the stories of average Christians and Christian leaders: massive tension. The tension exists because we all tend to understand and recognize the mess we're in, but we can't translate that knowledge into our "Body," our churches.

This tension has several sources; we'll discuss five of them here.

First, it can come from a broken heart. Some of us just have a gut-level yearning that spiritual Sojourners will find faith and a community that brings them life. I don't cry much. I do cry however, when I hear Kid Rock and Sheryl Crow singing about sleeping with other people while still loving others. Their words seem to be a mirror of the relational horror that millions of people live every day. I get teary when I look at my twelve-year-old, who is now going through the pains of insecurity associated with middle school, and I think of hundreds of her classmates who don't have fathers who nurture their souls or prepare them for life. I cry when I see stories on the news about despondent families or abused children. Other than these normal things, I also get a little misty during *Extreme Home Makeover*. (But who doesn't?)

Second, tension can arise from simple frustration of energy and resources wasted. We've worked so hard for so little, and we don't know what else to try. We've tried Graham crusades, Promise Keepers, Willow Creek Church, Saddleback's four bases, the "small group" movement in every conceivable arrangement, Alpha, 40-Days of Everything, and house church. Yet we continue to lose the people we have while failing to reach the ones we don't have. We often see this tension when working with denominational executives or pastors. They've put a lot of time and energy, blood, sweat, and prayers into their movements or their churches. It just flat hurts when you've given generously of your time, money, and emotional energy to missional efforts without seeing results. These poignant and honest words come from one of my personal mentors, a faithful, respected pastor of one church for more than thirty years:

> Hugh,
>
> I headed out of my house around 5 a.m. this morning for a nice brisk bike ride to the airport and back. I've heard it's good for me to do that sort of thing. Anyway, it's cheaper than golf. I was jazzed because I beat my time from last week. I even passed some younger bucks (a couple of them actually going the same direction I was heading). At 60 years old I still press to do my best. I hate coming in last. I want to win, do it better, do it faster. I spent $900 for my Bianchi; it was the best bike my money could buy, but next to my

buddy's bikes, it's a tank. Yet, I will continue riding, giving it my best, while I dream about that $2500 bike I'd love to buy.

I approach ministry the same way. I average a couple hours a day in prayer, hang out at coffee shops, check out bike clubs to ride with (where all the ungodly guys hang out). I visit hospitals, teach and preach, coach young men, counsel marriages, and anything else I can fit into a normal 14-hour day. I'm embarrassed when I think about how long it's been since I led someone to Christ. I've lost more folks from the church this past year than I've gained. I read everything I can get my hands on. I listen, not afraid to learn from younger guys who mysteriously seem to get things right. I coach church planters and pastors on the fine art of starting and leading a church, all the while wondering what in the world gives me the right to do this stuff. I'm well aware of the numbers. I live with them every Sunday. I try my best to be biblical and relevant, both in preaching and coaching. I'm dumb enough to think that next week will be better. Most mornings I will be on my knees by 4:30 a.m. seeking his face.

I didn't go into the ministry to be a miserable failure. Frankly, from all my reading, that's pretty much what I gather the younger generation thinks of us older pastors. I too had dreams of a better day, of a larger impact, of better numbers. Can I work harder? No. Can I work smarter? I'm sure I can and that's why I read, listen, seek his face. I'm not complaining or bemoaning my lot. I wouldn't trade my call for all the world. I just don't think that most of the guys in the missional church movement understand us or the situations where we find ourselves. The world around us has changed and we didn't change fast enough with it. The jump from modern to postmodern caught us on our heels. Can we still change? I don't know, but we will know soon.

Yes, we often need a kick in the butt (isn't that why we get married?), but we also need a word of encouragement. America would be in a hell of a mess if all the older traditional type pastors decided to give up, pick up their Bibles, and go home.

Sorry about the acid tone of my response. This is tension, but it's also passion.

Love ya, bro. Go get 'em.

As I speak for many in the budding new missional church world, I have to share that I no longer judge the faithful, fervent work of so many pastors who have pastored well but who struggle to find their place in this new world. They deserve to be honored instead of belittled. Without their legacy, we would have nothing to build upon.

Third, tension can bring fear. If we're in vocational ministry, ushering in anything new may cause us to abandon forms of church that have brought us great respect, self-esteem, and probably our livelihoods. Tension also comes when you know you can't go back to present forms of church, but you don't know what going forward will look like or what it will cost us in life, focus, family, or finances.

There's not a week that goes by that we do not meet a despondent pastor or a jaded Christian who has been stuck in "time-out" mode. Looking back over the past ten years, I can say I've spent as much time reevangelizing these people as I have with people outside the Christian faith. It is actually quite a bit harder to try to reconvince those in the know than those who don't know anything. For them, the discussion isn't about proving Jesus. It's about giving them hope that Jesus can or will still work with the church.

A few months ago, I met a gifted man who had just left a successful worship position at a local mega-church. In his own words, he said, "I just can't do the show any more." As we talked, it was clear that he respected the pastors he had left, and he still seemed to be committed to the idea of church. He just couldn't justify spending 50 hours a week preparing songs and spending huge sums of money on large worship and drama productions. He was yearning for time with people and was willing to work at Starbucks and live by faith for his six children instead of returning to his past experience. Six kids, the life of a barista, no clue how to survive, but a sense of never going back. Now that's tension!

You can't go back, but forward doesn't feel much better, because forward may not pay the bills or make it any easier to live the Christian life you've always wanted to live. It's a painful thing to watch, and there are no easy answers.

Fourth, tension arises when you see the structure of church falling, and you realize that everything the church stood on may go down too. Issues of doctrine, theology, and church practices all of a sudden come under critique. You may not know it, but there's a war a-brewing. If you haven't heard the shots being fired, just wait a few years. This growing undercurrent is more pervasive than you think. Let me explain a bit more.

Matt and I facilitate an international collaborative training environment for incarnational church planters and emerging leaders called MCAP (Missional Church Apprenticeship Practicum). This network is comprised of highly gifted, deeply passionate, and doctrinally savvy leaders. They can't get into our environment unless they exhibit a love of the scriptures, the church, and the lost. But we see some interesting trends in how they process some basic evangelical and theological stakes that we've driven in the ground and tied our success to.

For instance, they are convinced that people need Christ's atonement for their sin, and that people need to deal with God personally, but they don't feel that getting someone to "pray the prayer" is the focus of their ministry. They tend to focus more on providing a pathway that is conducive for the Holy Spirit to convert the person. Thus, they don't focus on who goes to heaven and who doesn't, but how to help people find heaven. They aren't sure all evangelical Christians will make it in, including many wing-nut pastors, and they feel that Pharisee-ism is alive and well and will be judged much more harshly than the clueless meth addict who hangs on the forgiveness of Christ while he struggles with his addiction. They don't put a lot of confidence in sermons or programs to transform a person and tend to prefer a good talk at the pub to influence the heart of a person. These leaders aren't that bugged by people sinning. They don't focus much on behavior, believing that if you can win the heart, behavior will follow. They think the homosexuals' fight for sexual clarity isn't that much different in God's sight than the heterosexuals' struggle against pornography.

The best way to characterize this coming civil war is to see the church in two primary camps. One we'll call "Jerusalem Christians" (those who see the person of Jesus through their traditions and the literal interpretation of doctrine) and the other "Galilee Christians" (those who see the Christian message through the person of Jesus and the narratives about his life). Often, Jerusalem Christians turn belief into dogma: arbitrary rules of life that people are held to beyond their common sense.

A few examples may help here. Jerusalem people are represented pretty heavily in the traditional evangelical camp. They hold doctrine so tightly that sometimes the life of Jesus gets obscured. For example, while in seminary my Jerusalem-oriented professor of New Testament said that Christian leaders should never drink alcohol. As any good Irishman would do, I raised my hand and asked the obvious question, "Didn't Jesus drink and make wine?" I was asked to leave the class before an answer came. This man interpreted other scriptures so that he could create a case for grape juice instead of wine. I, on the other hand, was focusing on What Did Jesus Do? Others may piece together some scripture and conclude that Christians shouldn't have non-Christian friends, yet Jesus was called a friend of sinners. Hundreds of thousands of Christians believe you can't get into heaven without "praying the sinner's prayer," even though Jesus granted salvation to many without one reference to a person praying a prayer. Even postresurrection, there's no precedence for praying a prayer as the ticket to eternity.

Galilean Christians are those who interpret the Bible through the life of Jesus. The Jerusalem people, therefore, tend to be more literal and conscious of correct doctrine, whereas Galileans try to develop a correct theological framework around the life and deeds of Jesus. Jerusalem Christians are more comfortable with black and white. Galilean Christians were forced to deal honestly with the grey areas. Jerusalem Christians strive for perfection in the minutest details, whereas Galilean Christians just want to make sure they don't mess up on any of the "biggies." (The atonement, justice, mercy, love, benevolence and advocacy for the poor, oppressed, and sinners, to name a few.)

You might be picking up our bias toward the Galilean way and wonder if this more "subjective" way of interpreting Jesus and scripture is safe. Shouldn't we just stick to clear doctrine? Remember, much of the doctrine that we claim is so clear is still subjective. That is why we have so many denominations and Christendom cliques. That's why we have so many church splits and dissention. By starting with Christology (the life of Jesus), which informs our missiology (how we live), we'll have a better chance of finding common ground with our ecclesiology (how we do church).

One church Matt and I were working with was known for being one of the better "Bible-teaching" churches in our area. The pastor went to a well-known "Jerusalem-based" seminary and grew his church because parishioners would invite their friends to hear the Bible taught well. A turning point happened to him when he came to the realization that he'd discipled his church to be Jerusalem Christians. They knew the letter, but they didn't have the behavior of Jesus, especially as it related to engaging the world. How did he know? Simply because they experienced so few new conversions stories. In a "state of the union" sermon, he repented for helping them become, as he said, "idolaters of the Bible" and for prioritizing head knowledge over heart life.

In John 5:39, Jesus challenged the Jerusalem followers this way: "You diligently study the Scriptures because you think that by them you possess eternal life. These are the Scriptures that testify about me, yet you refuse to come to me to have life." Translation? "You prioritize and trust in your own interpretations instead of coming to the real me."

As you reflect on the differences, consider these questions: Would Christians today be different if we only had the four Gospels to interpret? What if we all had to look at over all these centuries were the four accounts of Christ's life? Would we be better Christians on the streets? I think we probably would. Sure we would be missing a depth of rich theology about Christ through Paul, John, Peter, and a few others, but "What would Jesus do?" would not be a wristband we wear but the constant attention of our lives. We would live like Jesus! Theology is great, but if it becomes doctrine that overshadows or distracts us from the life of Jesus, we not only miss out on the Tangible Kingdom, but we become hindrances to it. This tension will only be minimized as we maximize the life of Christ.

Fifth, and possibly because of all these other tensions, we have a massive tension related to identity.

I was riding in the car with my daughter Alli a few months ago, and out of the blue she said, "I just want you to know that I'm not a Christian anymore." I figured this was one of those statements that meant something more, so I put on my Jedi wisdom cap and said, "Cool. Me either." It was obvious that I caught her off guard as she replied, "Dad, you have to be a Christian. You're a pastor!" As I asked her more questions, she told me why she wanted to trade in her badge. It was because some Christian kids at her middle school were making fun of a young girl who was a lesbian. Alli knew this girl and was her friend. Alli hasn't lived long enough to experience too many situations like this, but one is enough for her to question where her loyalties lie.

Alli was caught in a tension of identity. Before this event, she would have easily been able to say she was Christian. But now, when asked, she would be checking the box that says, "Unaffiliated, independent, unsure, and disenfranchised."

Identity represents who we say we are, and it is important in determining how we act. When you're proud of your team, your company, your family, you'll act proud, and you'll get off your fanny and work hard to increase the prominence of your group. But if you're ashamed or unimpressed with your team, you'll often not engage at all, simply because you don't want to be lumped in with something or someone that doesn't represent who you really want to be or what you value or believe in.

I'm not one to give up easily on two thousand years of history, and I have too much hope in the church to believe that it's too late to make a comeback. However, to make a dent in this issue will take time and millions of Christians to step up to the microphone and start acknowledging that my daughter had a point. I finished my dialogue with Alli by helping her remember how many Christians she loves. In the end, we each agreed to be Christ followers only. That seemed to work for both of us.

There is tension, tremors inside the Body and outside of the Body, some understandable, some just a feeling. Whatever the underlying issues, we simply can't do what I did to Matt. And now, for the rest of the story, as promised.

Since we were going to be flying fifteen hours at 40,000 feet the next day, we took the doctor's suggestion and acquired some Valium to calm him for the trip. Upon boarding, I was having visions of Matt freaking out and ripping the door off the plane in mid-flight, so I suggested that he have a little wine. The Apostle Paul used this option with Timothy, so I thought, "What the heck." The divine concoction worked. He didn't move for thirteen hours. I mean, not even a twitch of the eyebrow. Once I even reached over to check his pulse. Alive, yes, but not moving!

Just like many churches.

Unlike my attempt to keep the boy sleeping so as not to waken the tremors again, I think we're better served to be sober and address our tensions head on.

○
_____

Reflection

○ Do you feel tensions about your faith? In what ways are they like the ones we talked about in this chapter? In what ways are they different?

○ Have you noticed the Jerusalem and Galilean distinctions in your own church experience? How?

_____
○

4

U-HAUL

YOU MAY REMEMBER THE MOVIE *Castaway*. In it, Tom Hanks plays a man who has been shipwrecked on a tropical island. After several months without any human contact or hope of rescue, he finally tries to make an escape. He makes a raft and grabs "Wilson," his best friend, who happens to be a leather volleyball. They head out over the breakers and eventually make it to calm waters. Tom falls asleep, and when he awakes, Wilson is gone. He frantically calls out and notices that Wilson is bobbing up and down in the open ocean a few hundred feet from the raft. He dives into the sea with the panic of a parent who sees his child on the other side of the train tracks and swims with all his might to save his friend. While Hanks reaches out desperately with one hand for the drifting Wilson, his other hand is holding the rope that is connected to his raft. He is caught. The currents are slowly pulling Wilson, his volleyball, away from him and the raft. He wants Wilson to be safe more than anything, but not quite enough to cause him to leave what is security and what secures his potential for rescue. In the end, Tom is left weeping over the trauma of being caught between two things that are both important.

This story represents the true hearts of hundreds of pastors with whom we've shared our story. The tensions we described in the previous chapter are like a seemingly eternal pull between "on the one hand" and "on the other hand." In this book, we hope to give you some ideas about resolving those tensions so that we can move beyond them. But we should warn you (if you don't already know): Moving forward may be tougher than you think.

After Cheryl and I decided we had to reengage the tension that comes with being a Christ follower in a post-everything world, give up a relatively leisurely ministry post in Eugene, Oregon, and move our family to Denver, I had to fly back to Eugene, pack up the house, and load up the U-Haul . . . again. When I got there, some great friends were there to help, everything was boxed up, and it seemed the transition would be a smooth one. We had just about filled the 84-foot U-Haul when I happened to notice that we still had four rooms of furniture we hadn't even moved to the front lawn yet. I was amazed how much extra stuff we had acquired during this short restful season in Eugene. We all sat there, ate pizza, and laughed at the impossibility of getting all the stuff in the truck.

As the guys ate, drank, and tried to be merry, I was silently grieving the reality that some stuff just couldn't go to our new Rocky Mountain home. I was also a bit skeptical of my ability to make up pastoral fibs when my wife would, at some point, inevitably ask where the couch went. "Why can't I find the bunk bed? Where is the antique piano and dish set that Grandma gave us?" I didn't realize it at the time, but I was unconsciously living through a metaphorical illustration of one of the first tensions of getting reinvolved in organized ministry. (Now there's an oxymoron for you: "organized ministry." "Messy ministry" is much more accurate.)

Oftentimes, if you decide to embrace the tension and move forward, this is your first battle. To move forward, we can't keep everything we've always had. We have to pick what to take, what is absolutely necessary, and leave behind some things that have been important to us. What used to provide comfort may now only take up space or be a hindrance to getting where we need to go.

Pastors who get inspired at our missional church trainings often relate that when driving home they are filled with courage and fortitude. They're pumped up and ready to make any changes necessary to reorient their congregation toward this new frontier, only to be left babbling to themselves in the church foyer after one elder meeting or dinner discussion with their staff about potential "adjustments." What do we do with the pipe organ, the choir, the Awana program, or the ladies' aerobics classes? What about all these staff positions? What about this building? This office? Or all these Alpha books? What about all the time I'm required to put in at the office, not to mention all those meeting with other pastors and great Christian friends I have enjoyed spending time with?

These questions always come at the front end of your new incarnational journey. There's no way to avoid it, and it may help to simply realize that it's right in step with God's usual way of engaging his mission. He just packs light! He loves to trim off anything that would slow us down, hinder us, or make the journey more difficult. Sometimes that includes people, just like when he thinned out Gideon's army. Sometimes that includes assets, possessions, and material concerns, as when Jesus told his disciples to head out without tunic or purse. Sometimes that includes his work in us personally to strip us of those things that have brought us internal security, acceptance, and pride. Bottom line: The incarnational way doesn't come easy, at any level. Hebrews 12:1 says it this way: "Therefore (referencing all the great people of faith) . . . since we are surrounded by such a great cloud of witnesses, let us throw off everything that hinders and the sin that so easily entangles, and let us run with perseverance the race marked out for us."

We have to remember that the ancient faith communities that set a course to change the history of the world did so without church programs, without paid staff, without Web sites, and without brochures, blogs, or buildings. They were lean! The point of going without all the stuff is simple but profound. When you don't have all the "stuff," you're left with a lot of time to spend with people. Remember from Chapter One, a good missionary always starts with a Fiona!

In case you're wondering what happened to the houseful of furniture on the lawn, I gave it away to my buddies. Then I gave some final hugs to the boys and returned to the house for the last two items: Mitten and Milo, our two cats.

Now before I tell you the rest of the story, you need to know that I've never had a strong relationship with these two felines. For the move, Cheryl had suggested that I put each cat in its own carrier. But to save space in the U-Haul cab, and because Mitten and Milo are both from the same genus and species, I thought, *What the heck, I'll just let them share the same carrier. After all, it may help them to cope better emotionally with the move if they could be together.*

When I went to grab Milo, she saw me coming from the dining room window and began her normal attempt to elude me. Where she once had had numerous obstacles like chairs, tables, and people to hide behind, she now had only wood floor and corners. I limited her options by pinning her in the corner of our dining room. I screamed something nonpastoral and dove in for a handful of fur while she tried to get some traction—but she didn't. I ran to the car, carrying her at arms length, and threw her in the carrier with the force of you know who . . . John Elway. Only one kitty left, and off to Denver I'd go.

We just mentioned that the incarnational way will require that God remove some "stuff" so you can really go. But Milo's reluctance helps us gain some balance on stripping down too much too fast. Quite often we see leaders who get so disheartened that they react emotionally and deconstruct their church, people, and programs so fast that they have nothing to reconstruct with later. It would be like me noticing I had too much furniture, but instead of sensitively finding a good home or good use for the stuff I can't take with me, I just leave it there on the front lawn and drive off. It may feel good, but it never works out well. The key to reconstructing "ancient" forms of church requires patience, savvy, wisdom, and love for everyone in the family, even the darn cat.

Now let's talk about the other cat, Mitten. I could see that she wasn't afraid of me. She was sitting there on the first stair as if to congratulate me on my fine snag of Milo. I reached down and gently picked her up, gave her a few strokes of appreciation, and headed toward the rig. As soon as I opened the U-Haul door, she went kitty-schizo!

I could have sworn her paws stretched out 3 feet—like a rubber-cat version of Stretch Armstrong—as she kept grabbing for the outside of the truck. I couldn't believe how she was able to dig into pure steel. That is, until she sunk her claws deep into my neck and chest. After releasing her fierce grip, I wadded her up in a ball and in the spirit of John Elway, opened the door to Milo's carrier, and threw her in. The sounds that came out of that carrier were somewhere between hell and the south suburb of Sheol! (That's just north of Hades, for the geographically challenged.)

I pounded on the carrier to get them to calm down, but they just kept fighting. I had to take the carrier and shake it hard, like a can of paint, to get their attention. It worked, or I at least rendered them stunned or unconscious long enough for me to climb in the cab and get the truck on the road. (Maybe this is a good time for a PETA disclaimer: To you cat lovers out there, don't worry. No felines were significantly harmed in this story—they were cranky but not nearly as miffed as the human.)

As I made my way onto I-5, heading to my new mission, I began to think about all the unknown possibilities. All the new relationships, new leaders, new churches, and great experiences we would have on this grand adventure. As I went to shift into fifth gear and settled in for the long haul, I caught a whiff of something bad, really bad. Before I could get my wits about me, I heard the cats start up again. They began to spin around, shrieking, howling, clawing, and Mitten started to lose control of her entrails. Cat poop everywhere.

That was it! I pulled off the freeway (at the first rest stop, just 6 minutes from my house), jumped out of the truck, and slammed the door. The cats kept going at it. All I could do was walk away and go clean myself off.

From this story, you may understand that you can't just keep everyone together when you move forward to the ancient incarnational way. Some people will be like Milo. They don't want to go and make it very clear. Let them "not go." Some will be like Mitten, who seem to want to go but really don't. They are the ones who pay your bills if you're a pastor, give you nice strokes after your sermon, and who generally make life peaceful for you as long as you keep it peaceful for them. They calmly nod and smile when you're preaching what they want to hear, and for a while they even sound like they know where you're going to take them.

"Oh, we're going to be a missional church? Cool! It's about time. I've been trying to get us to do this for years!" "Oh, we're going to be really committed to 'community.' Count me in. In fact, I'd like to lead one." But as soon as you suggest that this new journey will include some genuinely "lost" people from the world in your church; or that they may have to open up their homes once a week to create small communities; or that you may change the service time to accommodate searching souls; or change a little music; or let "nonbelievers" be involved in church ministries and activities; or give up their first baseline seating spot, their position as women's choir post, or dive deeply into the life and activities of the culture around them, you'll see their claws begin to come out.

If you try to keep everyone in the same cage of your missional journey, you're in for some crud! Wise leadership requires that you steward everyone well; pastor everyone well; be honest with where you want to go and try to express what the journey will feel like, what they won't get to take if they go, and what it will cost them if they do. Then let people decide for themselves.

For church planters and pastors who wish to move their congregations deeper into mission, this is quite difficult. We used to be told that the number one indicator of a new church's success is how many people they have when they start. Now we say, the number one problem you'll have will be based on bringing too many people with you. Why? Because a good majority of the Christian world is unconsciously a Milo or a Mitten. They have good hearts, but they hate change, they've gotten used to being provided for, and many will take too much of your time and energy to try to keep on the mission with you.

Jesus was honest. In Matthew 8:20, he told a would-be follower that his incarnational journey may not provide a place for him to lay his head down. To the next potential follower, in verse 22, he mentioned that the follower would have to leave behind responsibility and loyalty to other people and social expectations. And then later, in John 6:67, Jesus asks his closest disciples if they want to leave, like the crowd who couldn't handle hard teaching.

How do you feel right now? Maybe like I did coming out of the restroom after cleaning off the mess. I remember being frozen as I stared at the front window of the truck. Five minutes ago, I was so excited about the journey, and all that this new season would bring. Now I just wanted to forget the whole thing so I didn't have to clean out the truck. *Was it worth it?* I wondered. *Is it going to get easier?* Maybe it would be better to head back. Maybe it would be better just to set the truck on fire, claim the insurance, and start over.

We can't be naïve anymore. This transitional time in church history represents an epic tremor of the unknown. Eddie Gibbs says, "The transition from modernity to post modernity represents a seismic shift that can result in churches becoming paralyzed in the midst of shock waves. The changes are deep rooted, comprehensive, complex, unpredictable, and global in their ramifications."

What this means is that understanding is easy, but change is brutal. It means that everything is affected, and therefore there's not going to be an easy way through the tension. No seminar or training will give you the answers. It means you can't necessarily plan for the future because the future is changing. Ultimately, the only solace is that everyone is feeling it.

Whether it be the Israelites' desire to return back to Egypt, the great westward-moving pioneers in American history, or any of us who want to see new land, there's enough pain and smelly mess to make you question going forward. We know if we keep doing church like we're doing it, it will probably only grow more irrelevant to today's culture; but if moving forward feels, looks, sounds, and smells like my nightmare of a trip with the cats, maybe we should just try to survive as long as we can and let the next generation figure it out.

Our hope is that you'll get back in the truck and keep driving, but drive wisely.

o

Reflection

o What both excites you and scares you about the potential of a new spiritual road trip?

o If Jesus were to trim down your Christian experience to his essentials, what would he remove? What would be left?

---
o

5

MOVING VIOLATIONS

SO LET'S SAY YOU are willing to move forward. You're packed and ready to roll and committed to finishing the journey, and you've braced yourself for some of the inevitable crud. What else could go wrong or make you want to head back?

In our experience, several consistent "moving violations" tend to make things worse rather than better. I've experienced most of them, so I know what I'm talking about, and I'd like you to benefit from what I've learned. We discuss two of them here. Let's call the first moving violation "Doing Church Differently."

Every week as I drove to our Adullam Gathering, I passed a sign advertising a new church near our Starbucks. The name of the church was "Doing Church Differently." The first couple of weeks I lobbed up a prayer for them. The pastor had come through one of our trainings; he was a great guy, with a genuine heart for people, but week by week I found myself concerned with the name of their church. I was impressed that they were creatively using a statement as their name, but I began to wonder if it communicated the wrong thing to the wrong group of people. It said to me that what they put their time, effort, and communication into is doing church stuff in a different style. It assumed that people were looking for a church; therefore the name would make sense only to someone who has gone to church and is looking for the same traditions with updated twists. But to someone who has never been to church, or who doesn't wake up in the morning looking to *do* churchy stuff, I thought this effort, well intentioned though it is, might fall on deaf ears.

As I once heard, "Doing church differently is like rearranging chairs on the *Titanic*." We must realize that slight tweaks, new music, creative lighting, wearing hula shirts, shorts, and flip-flops won't make *doing* church more attractive. Church must not be the goal of the gospel anymore. Church should not be the focus of our efforts or the banner we hold up to explain what we're about. *Church should be what ends up happening as a natural response to people wanting to follow us, be with us, and be like us as we are following the way of Christ.*

The second moving violation might be called "Circling the Wagons." You may have seen the *Far Side* cartoon in which the cowboys have circled the wagons to keep the dangerous Indians out. The cartoon shows the cowboys inside the safe ring of wagons talking to Indians who have disguised themselves by putting on cowboy hats over their headdresses. In this approach, we see Christians and churches that believe success in the future will mean keeping the remnant safe by circling the wagons and that eventually the hostile "natives" will go away and we can resume our religious move "west." Or at least enjoy our peaceful campfire suppers and sing-alongs without pesky interference by tattooed savages.

During one of our early trainings with leaders of a west coast denomination, one man blurted out, "This whole discussion is a load of crap. All these cultural changes you talk about are nothing more than a kidney stone to the church. It hurts right now, but eventually it will pass. We just need to preach the word!" Looking at the age of the man and the amount of Chex-Mix he scarfed during the meeting, I figured he was just too close to home on the kidney stone analogy. What he was saying was, "Christians just need to hold steady with the way we've always done things; the culture will soon get out of our hair and the real seekers will find us."

There are three primary problems with this approach. *First*, what we're afraid of is not just "out there." It's right in the middle of our camp. The same problems, ideologies, and behaviors that represent the coming "post-everything" culture are just as deeply seated in the minds, hearts, and souls of those inside the wagons.

Second, this approach increases the anger and resentment toward church hypocrisy. Not long ago, we all grieved as Ted Haggard, the senior pastor of one of the largest evangelical churches, fell morally within a homosexual relationship. This pastor was also the leader of the largest evangelical association in America. Known for his active lobbying with Congress to suppress the homosexual agenda, this man now quickly and quietly resigned for failure in the same realm he once publicly opposed. We all interpret these types of events in different ways, but one reality was made clear: Christians struggle with the exact same issues, vices, and sins as those outside our ranks. We had better stop trying to keep the hostiles out and start identifying ourselves with them and allow Christ's redemption to flow over all.

Third, the Circling the Wagons—a.k.a. the "Keep the Saints Safe by Keeping the Enemy Out"—approach only solidifies the false assumption of many outside the church that Christians are nothing more than modern-day Amish. Last year, I took our children to see Monticello, Virginia, President Jefferson's home. As we were standing in line, I noticed my two girls weren't listening to the lovely lady giving us the tour. Their attention was squarely fixed on a family in our group that was Amish. The girls were intrigued by their conservative dress and the haircut of the young boy, who looked like he had simply lain down in the field once a month and let the goats chew off a little. They loved the long, flowing white beard of the father, but they started giggling once they realized that the entire Amish family was wearing black Nike tennis shoes and the boy was head bobbing to his iPod. By the fast thumping of his head and the pucker of his lips, it was apparent that church-approved gospel had likely succumbed to P. Diddy or Green Day.

I thought it telling that these folks were still holding on to some of their values and traditions of avoiding the world, but at the same time they had succumbed to some "new world" ways. And there appeared to be no real rhyme or reason to what they accepted and what they rejected. My response? If they have Nikes on today, their Gap jeans will soon be sliding halfway down their fannies. It was obvious that they had not yet come to grips with the reality that in order to see Christ's ways enfleshed into society, we must be an integral part of society. *Influence doesn't happen by extracting ourselves from the world for the sake of our values, but by bringing our values into the culture.*

Moving Forward

A recitation of these common obstacles isn't meant to scare you from moving forward. We just want to help you avoid some common mistakes. Now, let me mention two people who may show us a better way to move forward.

The first man is a friend of mine. He started a successful church plant in the late 1980s, wrote a popular book on generational changes in the church, and eventually found himself a pastor at one of the largest churches in America. We initially connected at a conference when we learned that both our sons were struggling with epilepsy. Several years later, I found myself walking with him on the streets of San Francisco, where he, at great cost, moved his family out of an "upper-class" neighborhood, gave up all his perks, salary, reputation, and moved into the inner city with his wife and three boys. As we talked about him leaving his old neighborhood, he mentioned only that he longed for something more. I interpreted it as a personal quest to be able to spend time with people outside the church. He seemed to question whether all the time spent running a large program with Christian people had made much difference in the world. He wanted his family to experience life as normal people while also renovating his own faith and practice.

As we walked, we talked about his new life in San Francisco. I remember him saying, "The longer I go, the less I know."

That day, he went from friend to mentor, and he became a beacon of hope to me. Not because he had pastored a large ministry, but because he wouldn't settle for that as the goal of his life. He was an expert, but he had become a learner again. He didn't talk any more about church. Instead he kept wrestling with ideas about the Kingdom of God. He seemed genuinely enthusiastic about the small new group of people who were meeting in their living rooms. Instead of giving random numbers, he mentioned their names. His greatest pride seemed to be related to a Jewish family who had asked him to take part in their family gatherings and to people on their street starting to care for each other. He seemed to have his heart back, and in the process he helped me find mine.

Another person whom I think might give us a better picture of how to move forward is my daughter McKenna. McKenna is eleven years old and is gifted musically, but she doesn't know it. She practices for hours, singing, writing songs, and she always seems slightly afraid to try any of them in real life. But she does try them. She tries out for plays, and she solos even though it makes her so afraid she gets sick. She was offered the opportunity to sing the national anthem in front of three thousand people last year. Forget about *her* nerves, I almost puked! Fifteen minutes before her solo, she came to me with watery eyes and said, "Dad, I'm afraid. I don't think I can do this." As someone who used to vomit before giving a 2-minute book report in college, I recognized her fear at a visceral level. I grabbed her hands and said, "Kenna, breathe, and embrace the fear." I felt like Kung Fu talking to little "grasshoppah," and I didn't really think she'd buy it. But she did. She gulped and then walked out into the middle of the gymnasium, opened her mouth, and belted out "The Star Spangled Banner." You couldn't even hear her last phrase, because the place erupted in applause and cheers. I slobbered and wept all over the Camcorder and couldn't believe the guts of my girl.

These two brave souls represent many others who may help us consider new ways of moving forward into all the tension surrounding us. Such people are all humble; they don't rely on past experience or present ministry posts to define them. They grapple honestly with their financial stability and at times make incredible readjustments in order to spend time with the unchurched. Sometimes they get fired; often they are misunderstood by those they leave in order to go with God into the world. These types of people are the ones who decide not to go to the next religious leadership conference so that they can stay home and go fishing with a friend who doesn't know Christ. They leave the church office so they can do their work at Starbucks in order to meet someone new. They intentionally look out their window and see a neighbor and decide to act like they're going to get their mail, just so they might strike up a conversation. These are the ones who embrace the fear, breathe, and then walk back into tension.

Planter, Shepherds, and Settlers

If you go to a church, more than likely it is a part of an organized connection of churches that has done things the same way for a long time. Each denomination we work with has its unique tension points. All have ministers who would love the first few chapters of this book. They would agree that it's bad out there in Churchville, and they are willing to take calculated but painful risks in order to go, like the starship *Enterprise*, "where no man has gone before." They're what we call "church planters": the pioneers, the ones that are willing to be the first to try something, even if it kills them. They are the men of Issachar who understand the times and know intuitively what not to do and what to do. They are underresourced, misunderstood, maligned by the churches and pastorates they left in order to go somewhere new. Sometimes they come off as arrogant because they have become bullish, brash, and, yes, jaded.

Are we all like this?

No.

Do you have to be bullish, arrogant, and jaded to be an effective missional leader, or relevant Christian friend? We don't think so.

We used to spend most of our time with these bold church planters because we thought it would be a waste of time to try to teach the old dog new tricks when you can release the young hounds into new, unrestricted land. Yet, over the past six years, much of our work has been with existing churches and more traditional pastors who don't want to settle for irrelevance. They are men and women who deeply love people—the "lost"—but also have responsibilities to love the found ones.

The hundreds of pastors with whom we've shared our story love unchurched folks as much as our edgiest church planters, but they are also responsible to keep a church structure afloat, one that signifies safety and survival for themselves and their parishioners. It's not an enviable position. I used to judge these leaders as weak, or unwilling, or even worse, unloving toward the harvest field. But now I've come to believe that they are just as important as the brave, arrogant, pioneer pastors. They are the shepherds; the ones who can help the pioneers take risks. They are the ones with the resources, people, and facilities who can help out the fledgling mushroom eaters.

Would it be okay to consider that there are degrees of missionality? That some will be sent to cross blue seas, cross cultures, and go to the far reaches of paganism in order to find the one lost sheep, while others may just need to be sent across the street? Is it possible that God doesn't need nor ask everyone to start something new? Is it possible that God needs millions of leaders to care for a host of Christians who won't be able to make the turn into new forms of church? I think so. . . . I think we must. The transition within the U.S. church doesn't require that we all travel on the same ship, but we must all sail on the same sea. Even in Adullam, we have some shepherding types, men and women who've been in the faith and in traditional churches a long while, are solid students of the Bible, and who love the mission of Adullam. They support and encourage us, but they never try to take over and dictate. They trust our hearts and our mission and give us a wide berth to be ourselves and follow what we feel to be God's way of being church. They don't waste time complaining; they cheer, and they roll up their shirtsleeves whenever they can, to help when they can. As someone who has lived my life meeting folks at the crossroads of culture, I have learned that I can't sustain this life and ministry without the encouragement, funding, and long-term help of the stable caregivers.

Within every congregation there are people at every level of willingness, strength, and maturity. I liken these Christians to bricks in the understructure of a bridge that reaches out to the other side of the river. They aren't going to make it across the bridge. They may not fill churches with new Christ followers, they may not even be people you want your non-Christian friends to meet, but they can help support the old and new structures that will allow the others to go out.

Several years ago, while we were seeing quite a few people outside the church find themselves in our community, we were at the same time financially destitute. We were losing nearly $3,000 a month against our equity and considered pulling out of our mission in Denver. One denominational leader offered us $250,000 if we would bring our church plant under their denominational banner. We had been training their church planters and had earned quite a bit of respect from their emerging and existing leaders, so we figured it would be a good partnership.

One minor issue, however, came up. (Actually, it was the same issue that caused us to leave a previous denomination several years earlier.) It wasn't on the level of education or doctrinal or biblical agreement, or philosophy of ministry, or strategic planning. The deal killer was simply this: they had a ministerial code of ethics (extrabiblical) that forbade ministers from having a glass of wine with a neighbor. The denominational leader was grieved that they weren't at a place on a national level to change the policy. He agreed with our stance biblically, and he knew they would have to change this policy at some point, but not soon enough to help us.

I bring this up not to point a finger of bitterness at the "settlers" who held back a quarter million dollars over this. (In the end, it all turned out fine: we stabilized financially, and I got to have a merlot with my friends.) Instead, I want to point out that some Christians and Christian leaders want to cross the bridge, but their forms, rules, and paradigms for ministry don't allow them to get to the other side. To us, that is not an indictment, but a simple reality that so many of our present church leaders find themselves having to face. Instead of creating division and judgment, we must allow these "settlers" to make some incremental moves deeper into mission while they focus on building a bridge to new forms.

For example, a mega-church we consulted with for more than three years was considered to be a great Bible-teaching church with strong programs and savvy staff. However, they honestly accepted the reality that their church had grown nearly entirely from Christians leaving other churches. Over several years, we trained more than five hundred of their people. Nearly all loved our stories and philosophy of engaging the world. The staff felt that we had successfully changed the corporate mindset, but we all believed it would take ten years to see full-scale behavioral change. They have kept moving forward, fighting for every missional yard, but they also decided not to wait to get there themselves before helping others get there. They committed a large portion of money every year to help fund church planters in Denver. While they make small incremental moves forward, they have become a bridge to new forms. Although all their people may not be missional in the sense we've described it, the church is now missional because they are "sending" and supporting the "sending" of new communities into Denver.

The call of this book is not to get everyone back on the front lines of mission, but to get everyone involved in mission. Whereas some would say we need to move past our existing church forms, we disagree. We just need to see them as they are, accept their weakness and their strengths, and find ways to help them contribute. It is true that to try to saddle up the horses and head in bold new directions as a group may be too aggressive and unsettling to the good that is being done within these more traditional church structures.

o

Reflection

o As you think about the church engaging the world with more than just tweaks, what expectations do you need to change, delete, or embrace?

o

6

POSTURE

USUALLY, WHEN LEADERS START to think about the call of missionality and to personal and corporate change, they begin in the church parking lot asking questions like these:

Why is the church failing?

How should we do church?

Should church be small or big?

Mega-church or house church?

What types of changes can we make to our programs or our presentation on Sunday?

Should we build or buy a building?

How can we increase funding so we can continue at the level we are now?

What type of staff do we need?

We may also start with our own lives. Like the sailor contemplating what it will take to navigate into that wreck-strewn harbor that we described in our Invitation, many pastors and Christian leaders know what may be required to move, but they're not in position. Matt and I often get e-mails from people saying, essentially, "I would love to live out my faith like you speak of; I'd love to lead my congregation like you have, *but* . . ." Then comes a long list of personal, financial, and practical reasons why they can't make the adjustment that will allow them to chart a new course for their faith.

Starting with any of these questions is the wrong place to start. Pastors, denominational leaders, theologians, and lay leaders usually begin here. A missionary starts somewhere else.

Where Missionaries Begin

We must start with people like Fiona (from Chapter One) in mind—she and the millions like her who represent our mission field. We start with *their* assumptions, *their* experiences, *their* worldviews, *their* emotions. When we start there, everything changes: our posture with people, our livelihood, what we do with our spare time, who we spend our time with, how we structure the fabric of our lives. Yes, church is what we're concerned about because we're deeply entrenched in its minutia, but we can't make transformative adjustments if we start there and work outward. We must go out and then let church reemerge as a reflection and the natural outgrowth of our missional way of life.

Missional at its essence means "sent." The idea is the exact opposite of waiting for the Fionas and their friends to come to us. It's the antithesis of trying to "attract" them to us, our programs, our buildings, or our gatherings. The most challenging New Testament concept is found in Matthew 28:19, which reads, "Go and make disciples of all nations. . . ." In the past, we might have focused on *make* and the responsibilities associated with discipleship. But today the challenge set to the first faith communities returns to us: . . . *Go!*

Yet, going isn't just about obnoxiously or insensitively going out to evangelize the world, doing outreach or short-term mission projects with the hope of inviting people back to our churches. *Going* is just one part of a much deeper concept.

Missional has an inseparable twin. It's called "incarnational." The root meaning of *incarnation* means "any person or thing serving as the type or embodiment of a quality or concept." Specifically, it means to "embody in the flesh."[1] John 1:14 gives us the picture: "And the Word (Jesus) became flesh and made his dwelling among us."

The missional part was Jesus leaving his Father's side in the heavens and coming to us in the form of a human. The incarnational part was how he took on flesh and lived with us. Said another way, *missional* sentness is focused on leaving and everything related to going, but *incarnational* represents how we go and what we do as we go.

God could have sent his son by asking him to set up a Web site and download spiritual information to every billboard in the world. But apparently he knew that information about him doesn't help people understand or love him. So the *only* option for the Father and for us is to embody the concept.

This is where a missionary starts. And the first thing that must change is our posture.

A New Posture

Posture represents *attitude of the body*: the nonverbal forms of communication that accompany what we say. As you may remember learning in your freshman interpersonal communication class, the nonverbals are more informative and honest than the verbal forms of communication. For instance, on the rare occasion that I might hypothetically annoy my wife, Cheryl, I'll often ask, "What's wrong, dear?" She often says, "Nothing." Now, I'm no dummy, and I've learned that "Nothing" actually means, "Everything, you dipwad!" In other words, verbal communication isn't nearly as accurate as the nonverbal rolling of the eyes, crossing of the arms, or inflection in the voice; it's what isn't said that often tells the real story.

Words communicate what we *know*; posture represents what we *believe and feel*. Therefore, posture is the most important part of relationship and communication. Posture shows true emotion and the intent of our heart. When we are trying to figure out why those outside the church aren't interested in our "good news," it may have nothing to do with our message, but with our nonverbals.

If you're wondering what I mean, let's take a look at some bad posture related to Christendom and the evangelical church. Let's start with what every American has had to endure while flipping through the cable channels. Televangelists. Men and women who dress in gold and silver Hagar suits, peddling holy water and happiness, while always asking for money. We may laugh and pay no attention, but consider if you never grew up in church and only had your TV to help you decide what a Christian is. Scary, isn't it?

Add to that, the mess some of them have caused by making authoritative political comments that call for the assassination of world leaders . . . all while they pray. Is it possible that there may be some truth in their views? Sure. But posture isn't about truth. Posture is about helping people want to hear truth. If this leader would have taken a humble posture and suggested that his views may not be accurate or reflect the view of every Christian, or God, that would have been okay. The nonverbal mistake was that he made the comment while praying. That's like a professional athlete who has just won the Super Bowl lifting his index finger to the sky and attributing his win to the providence of God and the obvious "truth" that "God was on our side, not the other team's."

What about the Christian advertisements we find on cars, T-shirts, and church billboards? What do they really say to people? How would you feel if someone cut you off on the freeway, and as they flew by, you were able to see their Christian fish eating the Darwin fish?

I remember sitting out at a local Starbucks one day and hearing a guy honking profusely at someone who took his parking spot. It got so bad, I walked over to him and suggested he chill out. It got even worse when I saw his bumper sticker that read, "Christians aren't perfect, just forgiven." I, of course, referenced the dichotomy between his words and his actions, but he blurted out, "This is my wife's car!"

Advertisements by their very nature are intended to coerce thinking and behavior. They are needed when there is no personal relationship between the seller and the potential buyer. This type of coercion is expected when you're trying to decide what beer to drink or car to buy, but it's highly offensive when people try to tell you important truths without any tangible relationship.

Nonverbals can also come across in the words we use to describe people. For instance, the word *lost*. As a Christian man, I know firsthand that "lost" is the last thing I want to be called, even if I am, well, lost. Or what if the term is *unreached*, or *target group*, or *unbeliever*? Try any of these out on the streets with real people, and see if you can avoid a fight.

Brian McLaren, in his book *More Ready Than You Realize*, deals beautifully with the meaning of the word *lost* in ancient times.[1] *Lost* connoted something to be treasured, worth looking for, but just missing. Very different from our modern-day meaning of being clueless, spiritually stupid, or arrogantly anti-God.

Do you ever wonder what people think when they drive by our church buildings? I read an article today that reported that the largest church in Denver was spending $93 million on a Christian high school. I don't want to judge the motives or intentions of this investment, and I know this church gives a lot of money to missions around the world, but I certainly wouldn't blame someone for questioning why another private Christian school should be built in the middle of another upper-class neighborhood. If I wasn't a Christian, I would simply chalk this up as another reason not to be inspired by the Christian movement. You see, even our buildings say something about our true ideals and convictions.

Posture is important because it can either obscure the message of truth or enhance and pave the way for a clear rendering of the truth.

In North America, people don't have any sense of the true Christian message any more because the face of that message looks so unlike the founder. Christianity is now almost impossible to explain, not because the concepts aren't intelligible, but because the living, moving, speaking examples of our faith don't line up with the message. Our poor posture overshadows the most beautiful story and reality the world has ever known.

Sometimes I wonder how we got to this point. Why did pagan onlookers hold the early church in such high respect, but today's non-Christians view the modern-day church with such disdain? I think one of the main culprits has been our paradigm of evangelism. In the name of "getting someone saved," we have primarily focused on communicating a message of truth to the world. There's nothing wrong with that, except that we've prioritized the verbals over the nonverbals, the message over the method, that is to say, the proclamation over the posture.

We assume that if we can just get the idea across, then it will be up to the person to respond, whether we do it correctly or not. Maybe we also think that in order to get God's approving glance, it's our duty to share "truth," even if our modus operandi is "Obnoxious for Jesus . . . and loving it."

Focusing on what we say without regard to how we say it doesn't work in marriage, with our kids, in politics, or in any other social arrangement. So why do we think it would work with God? Do we think he is happy with us for alienating his world?

The idea of posture helps us realize that truth is important, but according to scripture, truth is not the only thing or the most important thing. The most important thing is whether or not people are *attracted* to the truth, drawn into the truth, and able to understand and receive the truth.

Consider God's instruction to us through the Book of Proverbs: "A gentle answer turns away wrath" (15:1). That must mean that God cares quite a bit that we be concerned with the "how" of what we say, not just the "what."

Paul shares his insights on posture with those who were coming to faith in 1 Thessalonians 2:7–8: "But we were gentle among you, like a mother caring for her little children. We love you so much that we were delighted to share with you not only the gospel of God but our lives as well, because you had become so dear to us." An expanded paraphrase might be, "Because we found ourselves emotionally attached to you all, we couldn't just preach at you. We knew you needed time to process your faith, and the only way to help you understand the big picture was to stay with you longer. We knew the message would make more sense if you saw it lived out in our lives."

When we focus on the message only, what are we saying to people? Maybe that they really aren't dear to us? Is it possible that to share four great truths about God without giving the listeners a part of our lives might communicate the wrong thing? Paul knew that a message without an attractive tangible person embodying and delivering it would fall on deaf ears or be lost amid all the other faiths of that time. What makes the gospel good news isn't the concept, but the real-life person who has been changed by it.

Peter also speaks of posture when in 1 Peter 3:15 he says, "But in your hearts set apart Christ as Lord. Always be prepared to give an answer to everyone who asks you to give the reason for the hope that you have. But do this with gentleness and respect." These early Christians expected that if they embodied the message, they wouldn't have to target people or go after them. They enjoyed the alternative of waiting for people to approach them with curiosity and interest because of what they saw these early Christians being and doing.

After about a year of being in Denver, I hosted a surprise birthday party for Cheryl. I invited all our new friends (about forty people) for a dinner at a local pub. Matt said that during the dinner, my neighbors Jeff and Jerry said, in front of the whole table, "We can't figure out what Hugh really does. Since you work with him, can you explain the real story?" Matt wisely focused on the "consultant" aspect of our lives while avoiding the "church pastor" part. That kept the dialogue open and the growing relationship normal. Six months later, while we were brewing beer in Jeff's kitchen, he asked me, "How do you forgive someone who has deceived you?" After about the same amount of time, our other neighbors, Steve and Jen, were out in front of our house hanging out with their dogs, and I went outside to be with them. Jen nonchalantly asked, "How do you forgive God?" These examples simply show that when you are as concerned about your posture as much as your message, people will move toward you.

In our Adullam Network, we specifically ask people not to try to be "evangelistic." We suggest to them that if people aren't asking about their lives, then we haven't postured our faith well enough or long enough. We're observing that every story of conversion and transformation happened without anyone being approached with a message. The message certainly has gotten out, not as our main priority but as our gentle response to their curiosity.

When posture is wrong, you'll always be perceived to be an enemy or judge. When your posture is correct, you'll be perceived to be an advocate, a person who supports and speaks in favor of or pleads for another. As we said earlier, our new post-everything context is going to require that we belong with people as dear friends for quite a while before they'll feel comfortable belonging with us. Our posture of how we communicate to them—that we are on their side and advocating for them—is how we enter their world. Instead of drawing a line in the sand and imploring them to "get right with God or get left behind," we step across from our religious side into their all-too real world and ask how we can help. This too, can be done with or without words. Instead of picketing abortion clinics, we re-posture by taking the girls into our homes and lives and loving them and their children. Instead of putting another slick saying on our church billboard, we commit two years to getting to know someone. Instead of advertising our faith as superior to other faiths, we serve those with other faiths.

The Missionary as an Advocate

To be an advocate means that when people are in need, they know that we'll be on their team, and that we'll be there whenever they need us, for just about anything.

About a year and a half after moving to Denver, I got a call from a man whose daughter played on the same hockey team as my daughter. They had come to a few parties, community gatherings, and even a church gathering or two, but they were just barely connecting with Adullam. After a rather exhausting Sunday morning gathering, I was horizontal on my couch with the nice sound of golf commentators whispering sweet golf lingo in my ear. Just before I slipped softly into the great beyond for my cherished nap, the phone rang. It was my hockey friend. I couldn't make out what he was saying because his voice was cracking up. I eventually deciphered that he was asking me to come over quickly. I told him I'd be right over and drove to his home. When I got there, he informed me that their oldest daughter had been found murdered in Arizona.

She'd been a normal high school girl, but she was tragically affected by the Columbine High School shootings, which happened during her junior year. Since that day, she had never been the same. She started to withdraw and eventually ran away. This bereaved father and mother hadn't heard from her for two years, until this day. When I walked in, I saw the mom bent over, bobbing back and forth. I put my hand on her head, but I could tell she didn't feel me. I then stooped over and put my arm around her and said, "I'm so sorry." I realized that her grief was taking her places that didn't allow her to feel others. I got down with her on the grass and wrapped her up in my arms. She eventually felt me and embraced me. We just rocked back and forth together for an hour or so. No words, just touch.

You see, advocacy is different from empathy. Empathy can be shown from a distance; it can be communicated through a card or phone call. But to advocate for someone means you are with them in their need, and you must speak and act on their behalf because they can't speak or act on their own. It is caring in a way that touches another soul, person to person, rather than trying to fix that person from a position of perceived superiority. Henri Nouwen put it like this: "The friend who can be silent with us in a moment of grief and bereavement, who can tolerate not-knowing, not-curing, not-healing and face with us the reality of our powerlessness, that is the friend who cares."[2]

Jesus, in a much better story about posturing as an advocate for the spiritually disoriented, was brought into a situation in which he was put between the truth of sin and the real life of a sinner. In John 8, Jesus encounters a woman who is caught in adultery. She had transgressed not only Jewish law but also the Law of God. She had clearly lived a life of sin, and the Pharisees are bringing her to Jesus to condemn her and to trick him. According to the scriptures, the Pharisees are in a pretty good spot. They have the law on their side and hundreds of years of precedent to stone her to death. Did she need truth? Absolutely! Did she need to repent? Of course. Did her sin deserve death? According to their law, yes.

Imagine if the religious elite would have had some of Paul's scripture to add to their arsenal. 1 Corinthians 6:9 says, "Neither the sexually immoral nor idolaters nor adulterers nor male prostitutes nor homosexual offenders nor thieves nor the greedy nor drunkards nor slanderers nor swindlers will inherit the kingdom of God." I'm sure they would have said, "There you have it, it's in writing, people like her don't get to go to heaven, so we might as well condemn her to hell now."

But notice what Jesus did. He physically postures himself down to the level of the exposed woman and advocates for her. I imagine that the posture of this woman must have been low, bent over, covering her head, probably shaking in fear, tears splashing in the dirt near her feet. She knows what's coming, and she might even assume she deserves the torrent of rocks that are about to bludgeon her skull. Why didn't Jesus just call a spade a spade? Why didn't he just speak truth? He is truth; he can't speak anything but the truth. And yet, *truth* bends down, adjusts his posture, and kneels near her. He's now at her level; she's in his protection. She can hear his voice and feel him breathe. She feels his hands touching her, protecting her, speaking for her. The religious leaders challenge him, and Jesus stands up to speak to them. My guess is that he stood up simply just in case some overzealous Pharisee in training missed his first point and was still planning on chucking a few rocks.

Then Jesus bent down a second time and continued to make some scratches in the sand. More important, he bent down to let this woman know he was still by her side.

This is an incredible story on many levels. We always try to theologize what Jesus was writing in the sand, as if that's the most important thing about the story. But it's not. For all we know he was drawing a smiley face. The powerful revelation is that the God of the universe—the only one who should have genuinely been offended, who could have postured himself as judge and executioner—literally lowers himself to her level and becomes her only friend, protector, and advocate. Yes, he does challenge her lifestyle and asks her to stop, but *not until he has postured himself as an advocate*. This is key. He addresses her head only after he has her heart. When people begin to leave, he doesn't speak at her. He actually asks her a question, "Woman, where are they? Has no one condemned you?" She said, "No one, sir." "Then neither do I condemn you." Notice what Truth, embodied in Jesus, did. He removed condemnation from her first and then called for behavioral change. He won her heart first by removing condemnation, and the rest was history.

When I was growing up, the idea of evangelism seemed to be the way we "stand up for God." The goal was to just "get out there and say it bluntly" and then run back to the youth group and tell how much heat I took for God, not unlike kids who pelt cars with snowballs and then run back into the woods to talk about their great feats of courage. As an adult, not much has changed. Some of us feel that if we stand up for certain political ideals or values, that God is up there going, "Atta way, Hugh. Tell 'em the way it is, straight up! If they don't buy it . . . let 'em burn! These types of people don't go to heaven anyway!"

What is happening here? Are Jesus and Paul in disagreement in how to handle sinners? How do we now interpret 1 Corinthians 6:9, since Jesus just let one of the condemned go? Read up a few verses in 1 Corinthians 5:9. You'll see that Paul is specifically challenging Christians not to associate with other proclaimed Christ followers who overtly live out their sin without remorse or consideration for the new life Christ gave them. He says, "I have written you in my letter not to associate with sexually immoral people—Not meaning the people of this world who are immoral, or the greedy and swindlers, or idolaters. In that case you would have to leave this world." Even Paul knew that Jesus wants us to be with this people without judgment. He informs us that we are never to judge sinners, that we're to leave judgment to God for those who are disoriented. Our job is to be like Jesus in the world: to help communicate God's love and acceptance and to win people's hearts through close contact and covering. Don't worry, when they hand their hearts to God, they'll want to leave sin.

Christ's example and his scripture show us that God is not proud when we prioritize our message over our posture. Jesus didn't, and we shouldn't. He doesn't need us to stick up for him; he needs us to represent him, to be like him, to look like him and to talk like him, to be with people that he would be with, and to take the side of the "ignorant" instead of those in the "know."

I wonder what would happen if our posture became that of an advocate for those outside the Kingdom? What if we set aside our apologetics and our theological arguments and just lived as Christ would in front of others? I wonder how God might lead us if we were more concerned about being a "friend of sinners" than a friend to those inside our church or denomination? My sense is that maybe people would begin to have the same feelings for us as they did for Jesus.

Changing Our Posture

Our main contention is that what drew people to Jesus, surprisingly, was not his message. It was him. His face, the softness in his voice, the whimsical look he gave the children, how he laughed, and how he lived. His message repelled people. Many people who were drawn to him as a man would leave after he let them in on the message. This is quite a switch for most of us. We try to draw others by soft-pedaling the message and end up repelling them by how we live our lives.

So how does our posture change?

Well, it certainly won't change just by reading a book. It also won't change through preaching, programs, or pleading. For our posture to change, our heart must change. And our heart only changes as we live among the people for whom we will eventually advocate. Jesus modeled it this way in Matthew 9:36: "When He saw the crowds He had compassion on them because they were harassed and helpless, like sheep without a shepherd."

If we as leaders aren't around people like Fiona, we'll never have a heart for them. If you go to Africa and hang out in a village of starving children, you'll get a heart for starving African children. If you hang out with the mentally ill, you'll get a heart for the emotionally imbalanced. If you want an authentic heart for people outside the church . . . you've got to be with them. As they grab your heart, your posture will change, your angle of approach will change, and the kingdom of God will be a little more tangible.

○

Reflection

○ How are you willing to advocate for people while they live lives that are in opposition to the way of Christ?

○ If you could no longer use words to communicate the gospel, what would you do?

○

7

THE 1,700-YEAR WEDGIE

AS I GROW OLDER, I'm sometimes blown away by my ability to miss ideas and concepts that are so clear. I remember a day, early in my marriage, when I had to go out to the shed to get a certain-sized wrench. As I entered the tool shack, I did what I thought people only do in cartoons. I stepped on a metal rake that was perched just perfectly against the dark wall. I remember being hit so hard on the side of my ear that I thought someone was attacking me with a crow bar. After I realized that it was just me and the rake battling it out in the dark, I stumbled outside into the light so I could see how badly I was bleeding. I then went inside the house and realized that I had the wrong-sized wrench after all. Back to the shed I went, where—believe it or not—I was met again by the rake—different foot, same result. Only this time the damage was to the right side of my nose.

An avalanche of thoughts ran through my head, the first of which was, "You've got to be kidding! You're a freakin' idiot, Halter!" Quickly followed by "I can't believe it hit my nose!" And finally, "Is it okay for me to cry?" This time I managed to gather my thoughts by leaning against an old couch. After my eyes stopped watering, I exchanged wrenches and headed back out into the light.

I kid you not: I did it again!

Left foot hits side of rake, rake smacks side of face. I remember yelling, "No *way!*" Then I threw in some contemporary form of the Hebrew slang, *"Raca!"* This time, I went down in a heap. Out of pain? Yes. But mostly from the force of sheer bewilderment: I had made the same mistake three times!

Maybe *your* face is swollen, too. Maybe you're feeling beaten up by your past church experiences. Maybe you have gotten so angry that you became the rake lurking in the shed. Whatever the case, we invite you to step out of the shed and into the light for a brief history lesson that might help explain why the church keeps tripping over the same rakes. And let's do it without blaming each other, our pastors, or ourselves. Let's put the blame on somebody who lived a long time ago, 1,700 years to be exact. His name was Constantine. However, before we put all this blame on him, we should recognize that there are many issues that helped build the framework of Christendom, some of which happened before him and some after him. He certainly wasn't the author of Christendom, but he symbolically serves as a good historical illustration of what we have been struggling to recover from for 1,700 years.

The Pre-Institutional Church

Let's go back in time before Constantine showed up and look at what was happening with the ancient church . . . the one to which we're trying to return.

The easiest way to envision the pre-Constantine church is as a fringe movement. Although the early Greek, Jewish, and Gentile Christians were deeply embedded in the culture of the day, they were pushed outside of what was considered "normal" simply because they lived such radical lives of love and sacrifice and service.

They were persecuted, on the run, without buildings or financial resources. They didn't have a Bible or paid pastors to help guide them. They were held together by community, the teaching of the apostles, and the Holy Spirit. This type of church sounds great in some ways, but it was also riddled with strife, doctrinal struggles, ethnic disputes, and that pesky problem called "martyrdom." This ancient church was, for many reasons, a marginalized people, a "countercultural" movement. They had clearly defined values that were repulsive to the dominant culture of Rome and the religious elite—Jewish or otherwise. Yet at the same time the church was intriguing and inviting to those who watched them live out their communal faith. In Acts 5:13, Luke wrote that "no one else dared join them, even though they were highly regarded by the people."

Now that's a unique mix. People were intrigued but intimidated by these early Christian communities. They lived at such a level of commitment to one another and to God's purposes that they freaked out their contemporaries. They most certainly would have done the same in our day. In fact, I question whether we would have wanted to be associated with these quirky faith-filled folks. We might have considered them a tad bit overboard and unrealistic. In much the same way as some might view the Salvation Army, we'd be glad they were around because they help people and seem to tackle the toughest of social ills, but I doubt we'd quickly sign up for membership.

Yet this ancient church literally turned entire cities upside down. Its members had incredible influence on the culture even though they were positionally outside the center of society's normal flow.

When we consider these strange Christ followers who were both revered and sometimes misunderstood and persecuted, several things should grab our attention. First, we need not be afraid of the world becoming less "Christianized" and of being moved to the margins again. It has often been the goal of the evangelical church to try to get in the center of the dominant culture. Whether through political efforts, community efforts, or church efforts, the world sees evangelicals as desperately craving a place of power in order to preserve our good, wholesome way of life. They see us fighting for morality by trying to keep our position in the center of the culture. They see us fighting to keep marriage between heterosexual men and women, fighting against gay rights, fighting against Islam, fighting to keep prayer in schools, and so on. I'm not going to comment on whether these fights are good or bad. I just want you to notice that people see us struggling hard to keep our way of life.

What we're hoping you see is a new possibility.

Will being marginalized help us change our posture and allow us to put distance between authentic faith and what people think about what it means to be Christian? Most revolutionary movements, whether the emancipation from colonial England, or the Celtic evangelistic movement under Saint Patrick, or modern-day civil rights, women's rights, or the fight to end antiapartheid, all began as grassroots movements outside the existing spheres of power. And all these small groups of faithful countercultural people did incredible things to influence their world from the margins. When we call for the ancient way of church to return, we are calling for a return to this revolutionary position, outside the center of the dominant culture.

The ancient church influenced the world not by lightening up their values or by veiling them, but by living them out in plain view of the culture around them. Their lives exposed and challenged the present value system with new Kingdom values. Several cases are noted.

The Value of Sacrificial Community

In Acts 2:44, we get a unique but challenging glimpse into the level of interdependence among the early communities. They operated like a spiritual "co-op," if you will, where any need that anyone had was met.

Two years ago, my lawn mower gave up on me. Or I should say, I gave up on it. I'm not like my grandfather, who still uses the same chainsaw he used when Kennedy was in office. For me, if pulling the cord gets to "cardio" level (burning more calories than I intended), I'm heading down to Home Depot to buy another $299 piece of machinery. I delayed a few weeks, allowing the lawn to get to "vacant lot" level. Cheryl said to me, "Either go harvest the wheat field or borrow Jeff's mower!" I said, "Honey, you don't ask another man to borrow his mower. A screw driver yes, a mower no. A man's mower is like his underwear; you just don't ask to borrow it." We Westerners are a funny bunch. Our independence really is hard to break, especially in regard to our material goods. I know we all love the idea of people sharing their wealth and possessions, but it would be a scary endeavor if it was normative.

In the ancient church, the impact was clear: "And the Lord added to their number daily those who were being saved" (Acts 2:47).

The Value of Confrontation

In Acts 5:1–11, we have what may be one of the most alarming stories in the New Testament, especially if you're a people pleaser like me. It makes God look like the Grim Reaper! Annanias and Saphira can be compared to a normal American couple who fudge on their financial commitment to the church. Everyone else was selling their possessions to provide for God's mission, but this couple skimped on their pledge. Instead, they decided to head to Home Depot to spend their extra money on their own home improvement projects. What happened? God killed them. What's up with that?

When we train church planters, we inform them that it really *isn't* easier to start a church with Christians. They are generally more opinionated, more critical, and generally don't give of their financial resources any more than pagans do. Each gives about 3 percent annually. As we've tried to navigate the issue of giving and mentor people in biblical stewardship, I just can't see myself impaling a guy and his wife over this type of issue. Cursing people unto death for cheating on their tithe percentage does not seem to fit neatly into our church growth handbooks.

"Great fear seized the whole church and all who heard about these events" (Acts 5:11). And yet, in spite of obvious obstacles to human logic, people still decided to join the way of Jesus and the ancient church. People still wanted in. The church grew in numbers.

As we've tried to navigate the connection between "saints and sinners," often the lines between them get a little blurry. Just as with the Corinthian church, when you create a safe place for anyone to move toward God, you're going to have a messy situation. We're often asked, how do you control overindulgence, rampant sexuality, materialism, lack of giving, unwise choices of young leaders, and other issues that invariably come up? Our answer is simply, "Biblical confrontation."

The art of "correcting" people may be one of the most critical disciplines related to incarnational church. Sometimes it's assumed that incarnational or missional churches tend to be less holy and thus are a relational free-for-all. It's not true. But it could be if you miss one key difference in how we've traditionally tried to straighten people out.

Historically, in attractional churches (those that still try to get people to come to them), we have confronted from the pulpit. We've given general admonishments to a sanctuary of faces with whom we have little or no relationship. Because incarnational practices are relational, confrontation is much more direct and affective.

One young man who was growing in his faith asked if I would marry him and his fiancée, who was also coming every week to our gathering and a weekly village. She was growing faster than he was, even though he had a church background. Because I had developed a face-to-face presence with him, I said, "I'd love to marry you guys. By the way, are you sleeping with her?"

He said, "Yes."

I responded by saying, "Joe, I know Carrie has really been growing spiritually, and I have noticed that you have been helping her to understand Christ and all that ... which I think is great. But now I need you to really work with me as I help prepare her for marriage. Sleeping with her is actually confusing her soul, and probably putting you in an internal conflict too?" My question was answered by a nod of agreement. I continued, "The success of your marriage is based on your faith in Christ, but even more importantly your respect and trust of each others' desire to obey him. Sexuality is the hardest thing to put in God's hands, but trust me, you'll be glad you did."

He quickly agreed and promised to enter a season of celibacy until the wedding. My guess is that he's heard a few sermons on this without much success. Incarnational confrontation works because it's personal.

The Value of Inclusive Community

In Acts 11:1–18, Peter is on a roof having a dream about eating "unclean" meat. God was getting Peter ready to change the way he views people, especially those "nonbelieving" Gentiles. God was about to radically change the face of his church, and it would come at huge social cost. People would now have to accept not only women and children (that was hard enough for some Jewish Christians), they'd have to accept everyone, including Gentiles. That's a confrontation nobody would have wanted, but still it didn't keep people away.

As you reflect on the values of the early church, you'll notice there's not much that reflects a "seeker" orientation or the desire to pander to the dominant culture, either religious or pagan. No effort was put into making participation in the Christian community easy, fake, or personally beneficial. In each of the cases just described, there are situations and beliefs that would have frightened outsiders away and made the insiders prefer being outsiders. God's strategy of challenging valueless values with Kingdom values was the way the church grew in respect and numbers.

As Adullam began to grow and Christians started to find us, we felt quite a bit of pressure to make sure people were introduced to our values, particularly our values related to being a "sent" community. I set a "two-visit" rule. That is, if someone came to check us out and I knew they came from another church, I'd invite them out and have what has become affectionately known as "the talk." During the talk, I'd make sure I mentioned a few things. Here's a sampling:

"I just want you to know that we're not a church, we're a mission to Denver. I don't feel any compulsion to feed you spiritually, but I will look after your spiritual formation. I believe you won't grow unless you live like Jesus lived and try to do what he did with people. This mission probably has nothing to offer you. However, I'm interested in finding out if God brought you to us, and what your part in serving this city might be." I go on to suggest that they won't fit with us unless they are willing to open up their homes and lives to Sojourners and participate in a missional community within the city.

As you would expect, about 50 percent of the people who get "the talk" don't come back. Deep down, I care deeply about every person's spiritual formation. I also believe that the sermon has a role in encouraging our community. I just don't think it's any more important than other aspects. My intentions aren't to intimidate or frighten people, but to minimize the consumer church mentality and to find the people who are ready to embody or live out our values. We really don't need more converts; we need people who are willing to act upon the basics that Jesus taught.

Things like caring for the poor and oppressed, the hurting, and the confused.

If Christians simply focused on doing the most basic aspects of Christianity, like "loving" each other, it would say more to the watching world than all the systematic theology we could throw at them.

The point *isn't* to take these three values and create a twenty-first-century church growth principle. The point is to consider setting our communities apart from the prevailing concept and practice of church. If we don't, we will end up spending our money, time, resources, and emotional energy on exactly the wrong things. In the end, we won't be able to change a diaper, let alone change the culture we're called to influence. We've got to find the courage to live bigger and be countercultural while remaining deeply embedded in the world.

Christendom Church

Now back to Christendom. After the fourth-century Roman emperor Constantine came to faith in Christ, he essentially wed the Roman way of life with the Christian faith, uniting church and state in holy and intimate matrimony. As he legalized Christianity, church went from a persecuted, countercultural movement to the state-sponsored religion of the people. All of a sudden, those cultural revolutionary Christian types got the parchment memo that they no longer had to act so "crazy." No more hiding, no more dying for their faith, no more floggings. Not only that, but Constantine sponsored and paid for a bunch of slick new church buildings.

Church suddenly became a place you *went to* instead of a people you *belonged with*.

Imagine, if you will, the president of the United States building all of our churches, appointing all our pastors, and then giving them a hefty benefit package. That's exactly what Constantine did. He appointed the first pope, which was the beginning of the Roman Catholic tradition. As Rome spread, so did the institutional church. The countercultural people were now drawn in from the margins and absorbed by the prevailing culture. Thus, their distinct values were watered down and in many cases lost.

A few years ago, I was driving down the highway and saw the face of a college buddy staring at me from the side of a bus. Terry's handsome mug was being used as an advertisement for a health insurance company. I called to say how cool it was to see his pearly whites so far from home. He told me he didn't even know that they "had his face." He also told me how many other places he finds his face. In magazines, billboards, and such. Normally, people would be excited for all the publicity, but for this man, it has become a bit of a problem. His first annoyance was that the companies didn't pay him or ask his permission to use his face. Most disturbing, however, was that they were using it to promote all sorts of things that didn't necessarily represent him. He was the poster boy for a gay men's magazine and an STD treatment.

As you can see, sometimes being known and recognized isn't all it's cracked up to be, especially if your name becomes synonymous with ideals with which you're not aligned. How many times have you seen something done or said by a member of our "family of God" and wanted to run out and change your name? The word for being publicized beyond what you really are is *ubiquitous*. Terry, through no fault of his own, had become connected with so many products and groups he'd lost his distinct identity.

As someone who wakes up in the morning hoping to influence people toward Christ, I now feel my biggest fight is to tear down their assumptions about what a Christian is. At times, sadly, I feel like the only way to help people see the real Jesus is to separate myself from the persona of Christendom. Even my eleven-year-old daughter introduces me as "My dad, the pastor, *and* he has a tattoo and rides a Harley." She somehow intuits that she doesn't want people to think I'm just like the other Christian guys.

As Constantine furthered the institutionalization, the church became ubiquitous. It was everywhere: in politics, buildings, and commerce. This only pushed it further and further from its original identity. The church was no longer defined as "a people *who*" but rather "a place *where*." Ministers became professionalized, which created a huge dichotomy between the clergy and the common folk that still exists today. When they went up to the bishop to receive communion, they would have to turn their head to the side so as not to look at the priest. Although institutional church began a long time ago, it is easy to see that "church" is still a building or place, and the clergy/laity chasm is as wide as it is long.

In summary, the church lost the inspiring values that were so powerful in capturing the heart of a person.

Seventeen hundred years later, we're still entrenched in Constantine's Christendom way of church. Church is the place you go to, and commoners don't have to do much in the way of mission because the paid pros do it for them. We show up at church to get what we want (which is feeding from a leader), not what we need (to feed ourselves and others). And if we don't get what we want, we head to the basilica next door because that chaplain is better at giving us what we want.

Although frustrated by the consumer approach of their adherents, the modern-day paid pastors don't feel they can lead the way their hearts tell them to for fear of losing a tithing attender. Often, the pressure is so strong, they find themselves frantically trying to update their presentation, increase programs to attract people, or lighten up the message of the gospel. Basically, we're just playing musical pews (and will the last one sitting please turn out the lights?).

The spiritually disoriented world is unconsciously asking us to return to ancient church now! They're weary of our rhetoric, the same stories, or the pat answers and structures of Christendom. Their ears are closed to the authoritarian approach as well as to the watered-down pop Christianity. Like Fiona and her Irish friends, a new and fresh look at a Kingdom with true and eternal values may be the only thing that Sojourners are interested in any more.

○

Reflection

○ What are the personal tensions you are processing as the church is transitioning from the center of culture to the margins of culture? What tensions will this cause in most churches?

○ Which of the three values of the ancient faith communities (sacrificial community, confrontation, inclusive community) would be the most intimidating for you to participate in? Why?

○

8

PARADIGM

OKAY, SO MOST OF the church is stuck and has been for nearly 1,700 years. But we must change. And we must change now.

Do you ever wonder why a battered wife stays with her husband? Why people continue to spend money they don't have even though they know they are deeply in debt? Why some keep jamming food in their mouths when they're already overweight? Why do people stay in bad relationships? Why are some people still racist? Why do people still drink and drive? You'd think the response to all these things would be obvious and cause them to scream, "Duh, of course I need to change this." Why do we keep doing church the same way even when we know it's in critical decline? Why do paid church leaders spend so much time preparing for a 90-minute service for Christians who have heard it all before? Why do we still call our message the good news when it clearly seems to be *bad* news or *no* news to Sojourners? Why do we think Pharisees are only found in the Bible? Why is returning to a simpler form of ancient church so hard to grasp? Why don't we change when we know we must?

Could it be that we have a systemic issue? That is, maybe it's not about why we must change, or how we are going to change, but the issue of change itself. Maybe change is much harder than we think. To help us make those critical changes, we need to look at the issue of *paradigm*, that is, the lenses by which we see the world and everything in it.

A paradigm represents how we view our world. It's like a pair of glasses. We put them on quite unconsciously as we grow up in our unique environments, traditions, and cultures.

If you were raised in the South under a confederate flag, your paradigm may have told you that God loved white people more than people of color. If you were raised poor, you see things one way; if raised wealthy, you see things from an different point of view. If you grew up in a suburban evangelical church during the past sixty years, you have most likely absorbed a very distinct and very neat and tidy theology. If you grew up as a Christian in India, you have a more mystical theology, and you see scripture and the integration of scripture in an entirely different light.

The problem with paradigms is that once they're entrenched, they're a bugger to see your way out of, and if they're wrong, it is like going out on a night ride on your Harley wearing dark sunglasses. It's just not safe. Paradigms therefore determine our routines or patterns of life and are reflected in our customs and traditions. The most entrenched forms become doctrine that we feel compelled to coerce onto others, even if those paradigms are fundamentally wrong. "The Bible says . . ." becomes our defense, even though our interpretation may be skewed.

You can see this issue throughout history. Just a few hundred years ago, everyone thought the world was flat. It was the paradigm. So they put up buoys just offshore that warned sailors they shouldn't sail too far past them or they'd drop off the Earth.

Paradigms can either propel us into action or they can shut us down and limit what we do and what we think is possible. For example, within the history of the church, it is astounding that Peter was prejudiced toward the Gentiles. He didn't think Gentiles could receive salvation. Even the most spiritually devout can miss some biggies!

The danger we speak of regarding the paradigms of the contemporary church isn't that we've lost our heart for the world or that we do bad church. The problem is that our present evangelical "Come to us" paradigm of church has not been an appropriate missiological response to the paradigms that exist in our world.

Remember all the books on boomers, GenXers, busters, millennials, and postmoderns? The reason we read these books was that we assumed that if we could understand the way people think and live, we could adjust our methods of ministry in such a way as to reach them. Most of the time, we categorized people by age, assuming that there were clear-cut lines of demarcation based on when someone was born. Now we know that it's just not so. There are some tendencies within each of these groupings, but if you've spent any time away from the church bubble, talking to real people, it becomes obvious that each individual represents a distinctly unique convergence of many influences.

The street you live on, the Starbucks or pub you frequent, the city or neighborhood you live in will determine what you hear. Boomers can be postmodern, postmoderns can be eighty-five-year-old bingo players, and twenty-two-year-old left-wing Democrats can be quite evangelical in their orientation. You can meet a strict evolutionist who believes in reincarnation or a Baptist housewife in Colorado Springs who thinks Oprah is nearly on the same spiritual and theological competency level as Jesus.

Can you see the danger of oversimplifying our methods? You might recall the story of the seven sons of Sceva in Acts 19. They tried to apply a method they saw some of the apostles using in one location to a demon-possessed guy in another location. Their hearts seemed good. Their expectations were realistic, and their efforts were notable. The result, however, was a smidge uncomfortable. Not only *didn't* the method work, but the demon laughed at the guys, beat them up, and left them running through the city buck naked. Now that's a bad day at the office!

Let's now have a go at understanding the three dominant paradigms we swim in and consider an old paradigm that will influence them all.

Three Paradigms

So that we can present an alternative Kingdom paradigm to the world, let's learn a bit about three primary paradigms that people live in and think from: Westernism, Easternism, and postmodernism.

Westernism/Modernism

This is the paradigm (we call it "WestMod" for short) that grew out of the Enlightenment in Europe about four hundred years ago (following the so-called Dark Ages). People in the Dark Ages (also called "premodern") tended to be focused on God. They built churches in the middle of their towns and generally lived to survive the day and keep God at the center of their worldview.

The beginning of modernism began with the Enlightenment in the 1700s; that's when the "lights went on." People apparently woke up, flicked a switch, and became reasonable, smart, confident, and scientific in orientation. Oriented around knowledge, this empirical worldview took over, and the acquisition of knowledge began to spiral upward. Human beings (not God) were now the center of the universe, happily adopting their newfound godlike status. They believed that through scientific discovery and human reasoning, they could handle just about everything, know everything, or at least figure it out.

Extreme optimism and confidence was the unconscious result, even if reality showed otherwise. The Industrial Revolution symbolized this long season of upward expansion in industry, science, and social optimism. As the European way moved west to America, we moved even deeper and faster into our Western ways of life.

However, for as long as we've experienced the benefits of the Western/ modernist paradigm, it can quickly come crashing to the ground. The attacks of September 11, 2001, were a classic example of the modern dilemma. The World Trade Center not only represented human prowess and achievement, it also exposed how superficial our confidence was. Not only did a mere handful of men and two airplanes take down what took thousands of people to build, but it rendered our entire country on the temporary verge of financial collapse. So it is with the Western/modern church. We act like we're still confident in our modern church to deliver kingdom fruit, but the results hint at a deeper structural failure.

Easternism

Easternism ("Easterns" for short) is the second paradigm we discuss. Easternism represents the thoughts, customs, and worldviews of those cultures that were derived from the non-Roman world. That is, anywhere the Western, Roman world didn't conquer remained Eastern in orientation. That would include countries dominated by Islam, Buddhism, and a truckload of pluralistic religions. Interesting, this list also includes the Celts of Ireland and Europe and the Eastern Orthodox tradition. Whereas the church was at the center of the premodern paradigm and man is at the center of the modern, deity or spirituality is at the center of Eastern thought and life.

Easternism is a radically holistic approach to life, in which what you believe about deities or your deity impacts the way you eat, treat the environment, and behave toward others around you. Even the most uninformed New Age participant tends to recycle, eat natural foods, respect most people, take care of her body, and pick up after her dogs with little paper baggies.

Easternism, of course, has always been considered a bad thing to Western Americans. But let's not forget that in our Christian story, including our Jewish beginnings, Christianity is completely, entirely, an Eastern faith. As we discuss this further, you'll quickly see how the American church can benefit from recovering some of our Eastern ways.

Postmodernism

The postmodern ("PostMods" for short) paradigm challenges everything that the modern paradigm holds dear. Most sociologists agree that postmodernity started to pick up steam in the early 1960s. After the assassinations of Martin Luther King Jr., President John F. Kennedy, and Robert F. Kennedy, many Americans felt that even our best leaders might not survive and the great progress made on the human rights front might be turned back. The political chaos of the Vietnam War, as well as the heightened awareness of nuclear arms catastrophic potential, caused those who once put their faith in science to fear what it could do.

The '60s were a time of questioning and refusing to allow Western/modern values to rule or to have authority over the collective consciousness of the United States. The government wasn't going to have authority over us, the church wasn't, the military wasn't, our parents weren't. It was a massive rebuttal to Western/modern values. Because of this distrust of political, family, and church leaders, "personal preference," philosophical freedom, and relativism took center stage.

Putting It All Together

We're now going to build a table that will help you see the tendencies within each of these three paradigms, as well as offer a fourth, alternative paradigm that represents a faithful gospel response. The first part of the table appears as Table 8.1.

As we discuss these four paradigms, understand that each category is neither good nor bad, evil or godly, to be feared or accepted. They are simply the way things are. You'll probably find that you identify with one category more than the others, but you may also find yourself picking traits from each column that you resonate with. Remember, each person is influenced at some level by the three primary paradigms. If you are a parent and you have children in the home, we can guarantee you're dealing with all three paradigms under the same roof.

Table 8.1. Four Paradigms.

Western	Eastern	Postmodern	Gospel Response

The First Category: Why We Believe

This category helps us understand how people decide *what* they'll believe in, which is obviously important if we're hoping to encourage belief in Christ. Table 8.2 shows how each of the paradigms approaches belief.

WestMods would say, "I'll only believe what you prove to me" (*reason*). WestMods believe in absolute truth and that truth can be proven empirically and logically. The process usually follows a linear progression with a neat conclusion at the end. In universities, or just sitting around the dinner table with Dad, we learned to debate or argue truth and learned that a good ol' fashioned tongue lashing, with a hint of sarcasm, is the best way to sway a timid listener.

Maybe you've been on the receiving end of one of these truth tirades. Still hurts, doesn't it? Suffice it to say, WestMods are driven to try to prove (or disprove) the existence of God and all that is related to him.

For those of us who desired to go on to vocational ministry, "truth telling" was the primary skill we prepared for. My Greek professor once spouted off to our intimidated class, "If you're not studying the Bible in Greek at least forty hours per week, you're not worthy of claiming the title of Pastor." For normal guys who excelled in their seminary education (unlike me), the expectation was that employment would be easy to find if they could accurately teach truth. If they got jobs, and became pastors at traditional churches, worship was warm-up for the Word, and the pulpit was the most important piece of furniture in the building, both practically and symbolically.

I was an apologetics major in seminary because, as an evangelist, I thought this would be my primary skill set and knowledge base. I believed that if I could have a quick and logical response to any question that might come up while witnessing to someone, I could win them over. *Evidence That Demands a Verdict*, by Josh McDowell, was my other Bible.[1] In my Youth for Christ years, this seemed to work. I'd take a student out to Dairy Queen, convince him of the Bible's reliability, and if I could get him started down the logical road to perdition, then I could get him to understand Christ, sin, hell, and, *cha-ching*...at the end of 30 minutes of dynamic, linear logic, I'd lead him in a prayer and head

Table 8.2. Why We Believe.

	Western	Eastern	Postmodern	Gospel Response
Why We Believe	Reason	Faith	Preference	Discovery

back to the YFC office to put another smiley-face sticker on the white board. Maybe it used to work for you, too. Even if it didn't work, you probably tried it at some point.

Easterns don't believe things based on proof. They'd say, "I only believe what has been handed down to me through someone I've learned to trust." Their beliefs are often tied to their ideas of authority figures or spiritual codes. You'll notice that most Eastern beliefs have been transferred through deep family, spiritual, or religious tradition. What they believe now is likely to be what their ancestors have believed for thousands of years. Not much has changed, not much is questioned. As long as the person in authority says it, it is accepted. No need for proof; just a trusted person to pass "the truth" down to the next person.

PostMods say, "I'm only going to believe what I want to believe. I don't need any authority because I am my own authority. You can't prove me wrong because I don't believe in absolute truth. I just believe in my *personal preference*." Although this may sound illogical and selfish, it may help to realize that people come to this thought pattern primarily because they feel let down by past beliefs or events. People deconstructed the government's authority in the 1960s because they viewed it to be untrustworthy. A twentysomething today who is completely confident in her own authority or her own moral choices, sexually or otherwise, usually has no reason to lean on someone else's wisdom. For example, many PostMods grew up observing their parents' marriages falling apart, which makes it quite natural to feel completely independent when making decisions about their own relationships.

I eat eggs now. Why? Because after hearing so many scientists claim that some foods were unhealthy, and years later watching most of them change their minds, I concluded that we can't really know, so what the heck, I'm having an omelet! That's postmodernity close to home.

GOSPEL RESPONSE: DISCOVERY. It's pretty clear that our three paradigms represent dramatic differences in how decisions are made. You may be wondering if there's really a way to influence them all. We think there is. It's our first gospel response: the *Discovery Zone*.

The Discovery Zone is a sphere in which truth can be seen before it is spoken, where a new authority figure becomes trusted, and where people are able to weigh Christ's values over their own. In other words, where they can choose to "prefer" Christ's Kingdom ways over their own ways.

Let me illustrate. In our current church context, it's not uncommon for couples who are living together to be drawn into our Adullam community. As is the case in most urban settings, relationships in Denver aren't just about sex or life together, but also about financial survival. We find that many couples become deeply ingrained in the life of our community, show signs of authentic spiritual growth, and become convinced of Christ's reality well before they change their living arrangements.

Now consider the WestMod pastor's approach. It might look something like this: "You need to tell them that they are living in an ungodly arrangement; that God is not pleased with them, and until they line up their lives with scripture, they can't be a part of the church." This approach makes sense if you believe the Bible is authoritative and if you believe that people understand the entire story of faith in their first month of "following" (and if you rip the Corinthians out of your Bible because people there were sleeping together). However, if you are trying to help people take ownership of Christ's values over their own values, it might prove more useful to show them the attractive alternatives. We must remember that people will always be interested in good news if it is observable.

At Adullam, we approach these types of living situations differently. For example, in a monthlong span, three couples who were all close friends and who were all living with their mates came into our church. All had become "every week" attenders and were involved in just about everything we did. One day I took the three guys out to coffee and began to ask them about their relationships.

"Hey, boys, tell me about how you met the great gals you're with." Hearing their stories, I continued. "So what are your plans with them? Do any of you ever think about marriage?" Surprisingly, all three nodded and communicated that they were planning on marrying their girlfriends at some point. They even joked about doing a triple marriage. Sensing their openness, I prodded a little more.

"Do you have any interest in leading them spiritually?"

One of the guys said, "Yes, that sounds really cool, but what does that mean?"

I responded, "It's kind of like stewarding someone's soul. . . . You know, the most important part of a person."

The same guy quickly asked, "How do you do that?"

"It's not that hard," I said. "You just work in the same direction that God is working with them. It's obvious that all three of your gals are growing spiritually and they'll continue to want God's ways to become their ways. So just don't get in the way, and if they are feeling excitement or discouragement about something, listen and try to help them get at what God may be saying."

They were quiet; they all nodded, and then the conversation moved on.

A week later, one of them called me, quite excited, and said, "Hey, I'm not sure what you think about this, but we were talking with the girls and we all think it's a good idea for the three guys to live together for a while and to let the girls do the same. It will help us all focus more on God, and we even think that not having sex for a while might be a good thing too!"

The next week at church, I went up to one of the young women and asked how the separation was going; she smiled and got a little teary and said, "For some reason it just feels right. I always had a sense that God had a better way for us to grow deeper. Steve and I have never been so connected."

Hmmm. You mean to tell me that without calling them to obey truth, you got them to obey truth? Yep, it usually works that way.

Remember, there's one thing that is just as important as truth, and maybe even more important. That is whether or not someone is willing or ready to receive truth. An environment of discovery is the only way we're going to help people experience an alternative opportunity. Helping them make a personal "preference" for Christ and his life will always be more powerful than bashing their values. This doesn't mean we don't get to speak and teach truth. It just means we're better missionaries if we let them experience it before we start debating it.

In this example, I had developed a long, trusting relationship with them. I had become a person of authority. They had been in many social situations with other young couples who lived in celibacy and whom they had grown to respect. They had been in our home many times and had witnessed a relatively peaceful home and marriage between Cheryl and myself. The Discovery Zone was in place.

The WestMod approach to leading the conversation with "The Bible says" tends to embitter and alienate. Interesting, when Paul warns parents not to "embitter" their children, he meant don't exasperate them by calling them to behavior without giving them the reason for it. "Just do it because I told you so" doesn't work in gaining their hearts. And if you haven't won their hearts, your views don't stand a chance.

Second Category: How We View Relationships

The second category is about how people process human relationships and social structures. We add this category to the table we're building in Table 8.3.

WestMods are *autonomous*, which shows up in how we dichotomize our lives into compartments that are unrelated and each distinct from the other parts. We can be a banker from Monday to Friday, ski on the weekend, put in an hour church service, have a 5-minute "quiet time" once a day, and generally keep very personal our relationship with God.

Table 8.3. How We View Relationships.

	Western	Eastern	Postmodern	Gospel Response
Why We Believe	Reason	Faith	Preference	Discovery
How We View Relationships	Autonomous	Holistic	Pluralistic	Inclusive Community

As a WestMod, I determine who I spend time with, how much time, and how open I'll be about my private life. The unconscious goal of keeping these compartments is to be able to control who we spend our time with and how deeply we connect.

Classic Western autonomy can be clearly seen in your typical suburb. Most suburban planners since the 1970s have built homes based on this value of autonomy. If you bought a home built during this era, you got a long front driveway and a garage door opener with your purchase. As you drove down your street, at the end of a long, hectic day, you pressed the button on the garage door opener from four houses away, and the gateway to your private world would open up. The goal was to make it inside your house without acknowledging anyone else in your neighborhood. Heaven forbid that a neighbor might be out getting their mail, but if so, a quick tip of the hat, maybe a short, military-style wave, and a second press of the button would get you safely inside your bunker without too much relational baggage. You lived most of your life inside the home or in the backyard, where, of course, you had a fence that was exactly 6 feet high—just the right height so you could see the top of your neighbor's head as he mowed his grass, but high enough so that you didn't have to make eye contact. Suburban planners knew that if you were not able to control your social bubble, you probably wouldn't buy the house.

This WestMod desire for autonomy deeply affected our classical evangelical experience. First, many of us came to faith in "stealth mode." I did, so no judgment is implied, but do you remember that after every, and I mean *every* sermon, a plea would go out for anyone who wanted to accept Christ to raise a hand, wiggle an earlobe, or blink an eye so the pastor could help you close the deal? No problem here, except the rest of us never got to see these transactions because the pastor made us play "heads-up seven-up." We had to close our eyes and bow our heads while all this cool stuff went on. After inconspicuously coming to faith, we would be invited into the side room, where we would be given a starter pack of resources that would help us begin our *personal* relationship with God.

Now, don't get me wrong, I believe that we all have a personal connection to God, one that no one else can create for us. But the ancients, the early church, and the Celts would have viewed this as a serious compromise to their understanding of a public confession of faith, which they did often at risk of death. The ancient Christians believed that God didn't want us to be in control of relationships or autonomous in our approach to him or others. He wanted everything done in the context of his communal people and as a witness to the world.

In ancient times, coming to faith was a wildly public experience. Conversion wasn't just coming to God; it was coming to God's people. It was such a visible declaration that people were afraid to join for fear of being mocked, disowned by their family, or killed. It really wasn't an opportunity to focus on the personal relationship with God, but rather on the significance of becoming a member of the household of God.

The truth is, if you wanted a relationship with God in ancient times, then you had to have a relationship with his people—many of whom you would not want to talk with over the fence in the backyard! That is the story of the entire book of Acts; no choosing of relationships or the ability to keep separate boxes of our existence. To be a part of God's people required that the fences come down, that eye contact be made with divinely connected people who were much different than you. No affinity-based small groups where you could meet with five couples who were just like you. No getting to hide out in your backyard. No getting to keep your stuff to yourself. No personal quiet time. You were now a part of a new family!

Easterns don't understand WestMods' individualism or their unrelated compartments of life. To them, such a life appears to have no integrity, which at times may be a fair assessment. Easterns are *holistic*. Everything—and I mean everything—is interrelated. What they believe about deity or deities affects the way they eat, treat the environment, or enter Jihad. They view their lives as already connected to every other life that exists and has ever existed. Therefore, they don't look to control social arrangements. In most Eastern countries, the massive population density doesn't allow them to "suburbanize." In China, India, or the Middle East, people have become accustomed to a much smaller personal bubble. The nuclear family arrangements are much larger, as well. WestMods define the family as a mom, dad, and 2.3 children. For most Easterns, the family means three generations all living together, sharing meals and resources. Sometimes this is extended to an entire tribe or village. This is why people of Eastern orientation are more hospitable than your average individualist evangelical. As I mentioned at the beginning of this discussion, there is much to be learned from our Easterns.

PostMods aren't really holistic; they tend to be *pluralistic*. This means that they desire that everything be interconnected but not necessarily interrelated. For instance, PostMods want to "honor diversity" as long as they don't have to share the same apartment with diverse people. They just want everyone to get along. Tolerance becomes the social norm, even though they don't necessarily want the raw community essence of Easternism.

GOSPEL RESPONSE: INCLUSIVE COMMUNITY. What's the gospel response to the three different categories of relating to others? *Inclusive community*.

In saying this, we risk a lot. There may not be another word that has been so overused, misused, or generalized as *community*. The problem with the idea of community is that you can have community based on anything. I have a friend who recently *gave* me his Harley-Davidson motorcycle while he was on a missionary assignment to Amsterdam. (I'm praying for him to have a long term of service.) I learned on the first day of ownership that if you have a Harley, you have a new family. All of a sudden, hundreds of people I had no previous relationship with began to wave at me when I rode by. I felt like a celebrity. I thought the world had all of a sudden got really friendly. Even gnarly looking dudes with ZZ Top beards and skull caps were treating me like their kid brother! But I also learned that it's not a community based on motorcycles in general. It's only about having a Harley. Yamaha, Honda, and Suzuki owners don't get the full wave; theirs is barely an acknowledgment of existence.

Thus, the problem with our idea of community is that it tends to be *exclusive* of people outside the community.

For the ancients, Christian community was unique, intriguing, and attractive primarily because it called for inclusion of *all* people. The Christian movement was the only place where women, children, and people of non-Jewish origin could all be together. One of the foundations of the early monastic movement was that the monks were a society of people who would protect, house, and care for anyone in need. Hospitality was a form of resistance against the exclusive sects of the day that sought to eliminate "outsiders."

The ancient church was not afraid of other faiths or people of no faith. They figured spiritual fervor in the wrong direction is still better than spiritual apathy in the right direction. It's like someone sailing slightly off course in a good wind versus someone sailing in the right direction with no wind in their sails. They welcomed people inside their community, knowing that the outsiders would experience acceptance and perhaps be inspired by the community's Christ-centered values.

Sure, the scriptures point to protecting believers from heresy. *Heresy* meant improper or skewed views of orthodox faith that could spring up from within the Christian community, or attempts by those on the outside who were deliberately trying to hinder the Christian movement. So the early communites were protective, but not exclusive. Early protectionism fought against deliberate attempts to throw off God's people, whereas exclusive community is bent on judging the intent of someone's heart and keeping the dirt of sinners out.

This e-mail may help us open up our idea of community.

> Hey what's up, Hugh. Sorry I can't make it to church on Sundays, I have to work. I will be able to make it Super Bowl Sunday actually so that will be nice. I also wanted to say you have done a lot of great things here, and it is greatly appreciated. My religious views are different than most and I still feel welcome among your church, I thank you for that. If I could sum up your church in one word it would have to be "open." If more churches were like yours, I might have checked God out sooner. My move to Denver has been great and I'm looking forward to getting to know everyone. I know it's hard sometimes when you have these groups of people who are so different but who are needy for family, comfort, and answers. You seem to know how to put people with people or in places that truly help them. I know I would never have the patience. Hope to take your money in a poker game soon.

Obviously, this young man is in process, but I'm thrilled that he feels that he can be a part of us without buying into all our ways of faith. I trust that as we continue to provide him a place in our community he too will prefer our views because of what he sees in us.

What causes exclusive community is fear. What creates inclusive community is love. In 1 John 4:18, there's a challenge to this exclusive posture: "There is no fear in love. But perfect love drives out fear. . . ." So, what are we afraid of? Weird theology, an occasional swear word, or the appearance of our friends condoning a sinful life? It might be good to remind ourselves that even within a group of typical institutional Christians, trained seminary students, and pastors, there can be some wacky theology and shady morals. Why then do we on the "inside" try to control the behavior and views of Sojourners? This tension is the story of the early faith communities, and if we're praying for God to move in our world like he did two thousand years ago, we're going to have to open our doors and create places that may seem messy or dangerous and will challenge our exclusive ways.

Because our cities are becoming melting pots for every ethnicity, because we have systemic family breakdown, and because there is a global cry for peace and unity, the church can once again begin a revolution of inclusive community in which the masses will want to participate. Even city planners are catching the drift. Front porches are being put back on homes, and suburban developers are literally "bringing the fences down." For now, in our typical WestMod churches, it should be clear that we need to do more than holding Bible studies with Christians and hanging banners on our churches that say, "Find community here."

Third Category: What We Value

We said earlier that when paradigms change, reality changes, and therefore values change. One hundred years ago, when most people had a paradigm that included a concept of God, even non-churchgoers shared values of hard work, truthfulness, loyalty, morality, modesty, and prudence. When the values of church and culture are similar, it's much easier to create a common space for saints and Sojourners to be together. This is why the traditional "Come to us" attraction model of church was successful in the past. People outside the church still appreciated our values. We didn't have to fight over prayer in school, the Pledge of Allegiance, abortion, or homosexual versus heterosexual viewpoints.

But when values are opposite, or even different, it is much more difficult to find a way to be together.

Alan Hirsch, in The Forgotten Ways, shares a concept called "cultural distance."[2] It can be applied to missions and church in the sense that certain people and groups are really close to the gospel and others are very far away. That is, some share much of what evangelical Christians hold dear, so all you need to do is provide a church in the middle of the suburb that provides safe child care, school tutoring, ice cream socials, divorce and alcohol recovery, and basic moral training, and you'll probably see some growth in the church. Whereas people who don't share the same biblical values will be completely uninterested in our homogenized church expressions.

Cultural distance explains why there is room for some churches to stay the same, but also why most churches will need to make radical adjustments. It all depends on who you are called to reach. If your calling is to influence those with the most similarly held values, then you can keep providing the same thing. But if you want to influence the massively growing percentage of people who are much further from the gospel, you'll have to provide, model, and invite people into an inclusive community that welcomes people with alternative values.

Table 8.4. What We Value.

	Western	Eastern	Postmodern	Gospel Response
Why We Believe	Reason	Faith	Preference	Discovery
How We View Relationships	Autonomous	Holistic	Pluralistic	Inclusive Community
What We Value	Security	Legacy	Gratification	Eternity Now

Let's add the values for each of the paradigms to our table in Table 8.4.

You'll quickly grasp that WestMods are going to be the ones who struggle the most with extending the gospel out into culture. That's because WestMods ultimately value *security*. We spend enormous amounts of money on things that keep us safe and secure: the military, local government services (police, fire, animal control), home security systems, retirement accounts, and insurances (car, health, disability, life, property, and so on), all designed to manage and minimize risk. Interesting, we didn't have most of those protections two hundred years ago. If your neighbor's kid was playing with matches and burnt your house down while you were at work, you couldn't sue for damages or make an insurance claim. You were simply out one house, minus all your possessions, with no place to sleep. No recourse, no ability to manage or mitigate risk.

This value of security is deeply rooted in our mainline church structures. We build buildings to draw and house parishioners who will support our structures. We wait until we're safe financially before we send out leaders to start other churches, and we tend to be much more comfortable sending money and people to overseas missions instead of sending our people to go on mission to their neighborhoods.

Ask any Youth for Christ or Young Life worker how hard it is to plug non-Christian kids into existing youth groups, and you'll quickly see how we have become addicted to minimizing risk. Homeschooling may make sense in certain parts of our cities, but when the primary purpose is to "protect" our kids from the dirt of the world, we have clearly succumbed to WestMod values, and left our mission.

Easterns value *legacy*. Their highest concern is not security but passing on their legacy—be it faith, wealth, or values—to future generations. We see this with our Eastern biblical leader Moses, who didn't get to cash in on his IRA but instead had to rejoice that the next generation would benefit from his work and sacrifice. Ditto with David, who was not personally able to build the Temple (his son got the job). Like

Moses and David, Easterns don't focus as much on personal benefits or safety as long as they are able to play a part in a long-term legacy. You might have noticed that when the 2004 tsunami killed or displaced more than a hundred thousand people in Indonesia, Westerners cried "foul play" and couldn't believe a loving God would let something that bad happen to them. In contrast, the Islamic, Buddhist, and Hindu people who were interviewed categorically didn't question "Why?" but were simply concerned about rebuilding for their children.

In contrast, PostMods value the here and now, which tends to appear as a drive for immediate *gratification*. PostMods generally don't fear death or afterlife; many don't even think an afterlife exists. So the highest value is to get the most out of life today. Reality is now! This may sound selfish, but in many cases *now* includes making a difference, helping people, and making the world a better place. The Peace Corps is a great organization filled with PostMods who are living well for today.

GOSPEL RESPONSE: ETERNITY NOW. The category of values forces a great question for the church. What values has Christ given us that would be intriguing and meaningful for all three paradigms? We think the gospel response is *eternity now*.

Ecclesiastes 3:11 confirms that "he has set eternity in the hearts of men." That is, God has created every person to desire meaning and hope for her eternal existence. Paul expounded this idea in 1 Corinthians 15:19, as he spoke of the hope of Christ's resurrection. He said, "If only for this life we have hope in Christ, we are to be pitied more than all men." He was showing that the power of the gospel is that it ties the two sides of eternity together and thus provides meaning for people.

The ancient communities were a window between the kingdom to come and the kingdom now. As people watched the followers of Christ sacrifice their reputations, their possessions, and their physical lives, they found a story big enough for their hearts. Searching onlookers would take seriously the God of these people and their claims of a heavenly kingdom because they witnessed them holding this life so loosely.

It's a common presumption to think that people today are overly selfish, consumer oriented, and unwilling to make a sacrifice or commitment, but actually the opposite is true. God created people to care, to want to find their place in the world, but the church has often missed the opportunity to draw people into an eternal perspective, one big enough to grasp anyone's attention. The typical message has been to be good, stop sinning, go to church, and wait for God to come back. Yuck. It's too simple. You can go about your normal life and still do those things without much effort.

What people want is an entirely new grid that encompasses every aspect of their lives. Values like meaning, sacrifice, simplicity, risk, adventure, benevolence, and justice will sell. But they have to be modeled, not just talked about.

In a second-century letter, Diognetus, who was a tutor to Marcus Aurelius, wrote the following about the Christian community: "They dwell in their country, but simply as Sojourners. As citizens, they share in all things as if foreigners. Every foreign land is to them as their native country and every country of their birth as a land of strangers."[3] This early church would have been an affront to our WestMod paradigm of security. The Celts would have regarded our safe and isolating expressions of church as aberrant reflections of the risen Christ. Who knows, they may have attacked us with clubs so we wouldn't water down their expression of faith.

Fourth Category: How We Influence

This fourth category relates to who will follow you. The question of leadership is really a question of influence. In the past, leadership was based on power or position. Today, leadership is based on choice. In other words, leaders used to get to pick their followers and tell them what to do. Today, followers pick their leaders based on whom they trust and whom they want to be like. The methods used by each of the paradigms to influence others have been added to Table 8.5.

WestMods have had quite a bit of success influencing people through *institutions*—through structures, positions, and programs. We got our cues from the hierarchical structures of the military, government, and business. In these institutions, the higher up you went, the more power and influence you had, because people respected your position. The

Table 8.5. How We Influence.

	Western	Eastern	Postmodern	Gospel Response
Why We Believe	Reason	Faith	Preference	Discovery
How We View Relationships	Autonomous	Holistic	Pluralistic	Inclusive Community
What We Value	Security	Legacy	Gratification	Eternity Now
How We Influence	Institutions	Tradition	Deconstruction	Modeling

WestMod's world of business cards, titles, years in service, expertise, personality, and position has had a profound motivational effect on people in the past and in many cases still does.

The church established a similar hierarchical structure, with clearly defined rules for who could lead, participate, or move up. To claim you were a "Reverend" thirty years ago carried weight with people even if they didn't attend church. Respect came out of position. People obeyed the leadership out of duty, fear, or guilt.

Easterns also tend to influence through hierarchical means, especially through the *traditions* that have been passed down for generations. Family heritage, honor, respect, and longevity are very influential and demand obedience.

PostMods influence primarily via *deconstruction*. Just as in the 1960s, many of today's emerging movements began out of deconstructing or challenging present systems. We don't always recognize it, but you can gather just as large a following for standing against something as you can by standing for something. Most revolutions happen because the common, oppressed, or disenfranchised people rise up against an existing government, regime, institution, or dictator. The same could be said for what is happening within some church institutions. Many of the new ideals about church come from critiques of present forms. Some of this is good and necessary and will likely help the church find balance in the midst of a wide-swinging cultural pendulum.

GOSPEL RESPONSE: MODELING. Although all three of these methods of influence still draw followers, there is a fourth way that most closely aligns us with the ancient gospel. We identify it as *modeling*.

When you look at the influence that Jesus had on billions of people over the centuries, you see that it can all be traced back to how he influenced twelve, then seventy, then 120 followers. His primary mode of moving people was to facilitate a big classroom of "show and tell." There was great power in his words, but his following came from the way he modeled Kingdom life. He simply lived a different story and invited people to observe. And then, as they were drawn to him, he communicated about a new Kingdom and offered people entrance into it.

I never tell people I'm a pastor any more, and I rarely even acknowledge I'm a Christian unless they give me time to explain. I don't believe I have any power or prestige from my position. In fact, I think it puts me a few yards behind the line of scrimmage. I don't argue philosophy or debate alternative religious viewpoints. I don't point a finger at the traditional church and say we're doing something "anti-church." I simply put pressure on myself to live in such a way that people want to be with me, and then hope others will follow in our way. If no one is following, then I assume it's because of me.

During our first church plant in Portland, I came home from a normal ministry day, and while I was having a cup of coffee with my wife, she began to challenge me on my crankiness. It wasn't just about me being an ogre that day. She seemed to be saying that there was a deeper problem with my level of stress and how it was being played out in our family and marriage. Adding to her list of concerns, she mentioned that my oldest daughter, who was six at the time, had said, "Dad sucks!" Now, I know where the word comes from, and how it's been generalized down to simply mean "Dad's no fun," but it still seemed a bit overstated. So I called all the kids in for a family meeting. I asked them, "Mom says that you guys think I suck. Am I really that bad?" They all nodded and four-year-old McKenna said, "Yep, you suck."

Cheryl later communicated that she married me because I used to be the "fun guy." But that since we had been in pastoral ministry, I didn't really turn her crank any more. She said, "I'm not going to divorce you, but just so you know, I'm not really enjoying living with you."

As a pastor and a parent, I know the stats are stacked against my kids wanting to follow my faith. Somehow the leaders of the good news have become consistently *bad news* to their spouses and children, and I feel the most pressure to model the Kingdom from within my own house. If I'm not an inspiring person, I may not even influence my own family, let alone people outside the church. So what did I do? I began to "model up" and change. (Still working on it, by the way.)

Our first year in Denver, my wife met a lady named Teresa. She had a daughter Muriel (from a previous relationship) and was now unhappily married to a guy named Jim. As such, Jim and Muriel didn't have much of a relationship. I began to notice that Teresa and Muriel were at our home a lot for several months in a row. One night Muriel and I were in the kitchen while Cheryl and Teresa were in the dining room. She looked at me and said, quite seriously, "I love you, Hugh." I knew she was communicating her heart, and I teared up a bit and said, "I love you, too, Muriel." Teresa overheard and stopped talking to Cheryl. After Muriel went upstairs to play with my daughter, Teresa started to talk about moving across town to live near us.

"I feel that if we don't spend more time with your family," she said, "our family is going to fall apart. There's something about the way you do life and God that we need."

So we offered to let them stay in our home while they looked for a place to live. I'll come back to the story later, but for now, you can see that the best and most natural way to win someone's heart is to model a way of life that's attractive to them.

In old Christendom, leaders got to pick their followers. In the post-everything, no-authority world, followers now choose their leaders. They won't be picking leaders based on the leaders' ability to preach or organize a religious institution. They will be following people they want to be with and live like.

Fifth Category: How We Measure Success

Finally, what will be the new report card for the church? How should we measure success to know if we're on the right track? Individually, how do we know if we're pleasing God? We complete our table with the approaches of the three paradigms and the gospel response appearing in Table 8.6.

WestMods tend to focus on an end *product*. They like to compete, conquer, take over, and beat the next guy. They like to acquire assets, complete projects, and be noticed for the work they've done. In church, this means that WestMod report cards measure the number of people attending, size of buildings, annual budgets, how much they give to missions, and how many people get saved.

As an evangelist, I used to have a "two-coffee rule." I felt that if I took someone out for coffee twice and I couldn't get them to pray the prayer or at least show some interest in God, I assumed that they were rebellious, pagan, defiant God haters, and I'd move on to the next one. I know there's not supposed to be any tears when we get to heaven, but I can't help but wonder what God is going to do with guys like me. There must at least be a basement floor where all the WestMod-evangelist types have

Table 8.6. How We Measure Success.

	Western	Eastern	Postmodern	Gospel Response
Why We Believe	Reason	Faith	Preference	Discovery
How We View Relationships	Autonomous	Holistic	Pluralistic	Inclusive Community
What We Value	Security	Legacy	Gratification	Eternity
How We Influence	Institutions	Tradition	Deconstruction	Modeling
How We Measure Success	**Product**	**Process**	**Justification**	**Transformation**

to go for at least a hundred thousand years. (Our punishment: trying to lead each other to Christ!)

As Matt and I work with church planters and denominational leaders, we consistently see tension because of misguided report cards. Often a young, vibrant, gifted church plant couple will take off on a risky endeavor to incarnate themselves into a city and begin to lay a good relational base for their eventual church plant, only to be snuffed out after twelve months because the heavies at the top don't think they're "succeeding." The pain of judging ministry success based on a report card is damaging to everyone.

We often have to remind people that we took nearly two full years just to develop relational credibility before we officially called ourselves a church. Most denominations we know would have pulled the plug on us, too.

Easterns by nature tend to be more focused on the *process*. Success is measured in the small steps forward and the experience gained through the struggle. They value all the little improvements made along a designated path. Sure, some of their targets are a bit nebulous, but nonetheless one positive Eastern idea is that the end result is not as important as what is happening in the person along the way. There's a relaxed patience and trust in God's process rather than a salesman-like urgency to hurry up and close the deal.

PostMods tend to focus success around the greater good of the universe and personal *justification*. If they have peace of mind, a good reason to wake up in the morning, and live in a community that shares their outlook, they're pretty fulfilled. Whereas, WestMods generally live to work, PostMods tend to work to live, and they live well. Both Easterns and PostMods react negatively to anything church related that looks too canned or appears to be a product or program.

GOSPEL RESPONSE: TRANSFORMATION. So what does a gospel report card track? Pretty simple: it's about *transformation*. Yes, that's another well-used word, but at least we know the point is not about increasing our knowledge or what we produce. It speaks more to the observable changes that take place over an extended period of time within a person, neighborhood, or nation. It's not to be mistaken as the moment of conversion, when transformation begins, but the continual process of being more converted to Christ and seeing people make small but significant steps deeper into his Kingdom. Yes, transformation can be difficult to identify, qualify, or quantify, but if you look at people and the world the way Christ does, it will be obvious where God is at work in the transformation process.

My neighbors Steve and Jen have become a very important part of our church. I first met Steve when I was unloading my U-Haul to move into our home and he came over and volunteered to help. During the first year, I prayed a lot about Steve and Jen. I knew they had some church background, but it was obvious that they had "put in their time" and were enjoying a break. As we grew closer, my heart and desire for them to begin a new season with God emerged. I found myself looking for opportunities just to talk. When I would see them outside throwing the ball to their dogs, I would walk outside, hoping to get to know them better. Steve would invite me to play poker with his friends, and we would invite them and their friends to our community gatherings, parties, and spontaneous dinners.

One day Steve asked me to help him build a deck on the back of his house. I figured it would be a two-day job and maybe give us some good chat time. I also did it because, as a recovering WestMod, I'm desperate to finish something tangible. What Steve didn't tell me was that this deck was going be big enough to land a Huey helicopter on.

As we got into the job, one week went by, then two weeks, then . . . you know how things like that go. One day, while Steve was at work, I went over to his backyard and began driving screws into the deck by myself. As I was bent over, being "faithful," I felt a warm sensation on the back of my leg. It wasn't the warmth of the Holy Spirit descending on me. It was Ruger, their 90-pound black Lab, "marking his territory." Apparently, I was his now!

A month before we began the deck project I had been in Scotland being a really "successful" minister. Now I was getting peed on, pondering why I had just spent three weeks of my life helping a friend build a deck instead of acting like an internationally known-traveling-consultant-minister-who-ought-to-be-building-my-own-church kind of guy. The only answer was that God had put this before me to do. I was just being faithful. And I really liked Steve and Jen and found it good for my soul to stare at a 2 by 6 all day.

Steve and Jen have been with us now for three years. Success isn't that they have found a spiritual home with us. It's all the little steps along the way that let me know that God has been involved with us, transforming each of us in his own way and in his own timing. It's all the little conversations, and the subtle growth in our relationship, as well as the change in myself. Not long ago, I got to baptize Steve's sister, who has also found faith and home with Adullam. If I had judged my successfulness or failure at month twelve or month twenty-four, I would have quit or been shut down. Incarnational life is going to feel different, and incarnational growth will look different. It typically takes much time and patience.

The point of this chapter was not to get you to try to categorize your friends so that you could "reach them." The point here is to help you see five gospel responses and a new, fourth paradigm that will help us influence the three existing paradigms.

A quick recap may help us pull it all together. The incarnational big-story gospel will require a place of *discovery*, where people will be able to see the truth before they hear about it. This place will not be a location but a *community* of people who are inclusive of everyone. These people will be making eternity attractive by how they live such selfless lives now, and will be *modeling* life in a New Kingdom in ways that will make it easy for other people to give it a try. People like this aren't desperate to convert everyone; they are desperate to be like Christ and to be where Christ is. Their heartbeat to be transformed into the image of Christ, and to pray and work for little specks of transformation in everyone and everything they touch. Success is faithfulness. The rest is up to God.

○

Reflection

- ○ Which of the three paradigms (Western/Eastern/postmodern) do you identify with?
- ○ Which of the five gospel responses do you most identify with and/or struggle with?

○

9

JIPPED

DO YOU REMEMBER THE WORD *jipped*? It's not in my dictionary,* but I think it's one of the best words I've ever heard, kind of like *ubiquitous, caveat,* or *robust*—words that not only feel good rolling off your tongue but that carry a lot of meaning. To me, *jipped* means to get short-sheeted, shortchanged, ripped off, dissed, deceived, or intentionally screwed.

I remember the first time I got jipped. I was seven, and I was at a local ice cream shop in Chicago. I had ordered one scoop of chocolate ice cream on a waffle cone. When the lady handed it to me, I remember having to stick my head all the way down into the waffle cone to find my ice cream. My friend yelled, "Man, you got jipped." It was the first time I'd heard the word, and I immediately forgot about my lack of ice cream and just sat there basking in how cool the word sounded. I recall riding my bike all the way home, saying "jipped" about forty times. After that, I started to say it to everyone. My mom grounded me because I used it so much around the house.

---

*My editor informed me that there's a reason *that word* isn't in most dictionaries. The word is actually spelled "gypped," which *is* in the dictionary. It is derived from the word *gypsies* and refers to the assumed gypsy practice of cheating people by "gypping" them. For the sake of Christian love, let's pretend the first paragraph of the chapter is correct so we don't demean any Romani people.

"HughTom, clean your room."

"Oh, man, that's jipped."

After she scooped me some dinner, I'd yell, "Man, I got jipped," just to get to use the word. This went on for few months, until I discovered the word *chick*.

Jipped went on vacation until my freshman year in college. It made its return when I was visiting a charismatic church by our campus. I remember being floored as the pastor talked about the Holy Spirit and its active working in our lives. While walking back to the campus, my friend, concerned about how I would process my first charismatic church experience, asked, "What did you think?" I'm sure he wanted me to comment on the old farmer dancing in the aisles and the lady singing a prophecy about "eagles and vipers" in the middle of the offertory. I didn't comment on that. I said, "I got jipped."

"What do you mean?" he asked.

I went on to tell him that in twelve years of being a Christian, I had never heard one person or pastor mention anything about this Holy Spirit guy or his pet bird.

Seriously, I had never been taught about one of the primary aspects of God! I just kept mumbling, "I got jipped." The next time I remember being jipped was in 2002. I was reading Dallas Willard's *Divine Conspiracy*. In this great work, Dallas cracks wide open the concept of the gospel and reminds us that it was never just "the gospel." It is the "Gospel of the Kingdom of God." That is, the gospel was about something really big, something different, and something that is to be experienced, not just spoken about. This gospel, according to Dallas, is about an aspect of God's divine life that is available to us now, not just after death.[1] After reading and seeing the gospel in an entirely new light, my heart started to race, and I sprang out of my chair and yelled, "Dog gonnit . . . I got jipped again!"

The Short-Sheeted Gospel

Do you think it might be possible that the primary reason Christianity in the West is in such marked decline is simply due to the fact that we don't know what the gospel is? I know that sounds akin to telling professional basketball players that they don't know how to dribble, or a librarian that he doesn't read very well. But the church's results of getting positive responses out of our gospel presentations begs the question, "Do we actually know what the gospel is?"

About five years ago, I was in Sydney, Australia, working with about twelve young church planting teams. These were very bright, attractive, nontraditional-looking leaders. The first thing I asked was, "Why are you planting your church?" I gave them a couple of minutes to think and write down their responses. When we came back together, I asked them to share.

Their unanimous response was, "So that people will go to heaven."

"Fine," I said. "Now describe how people are going to get to heaven."

After some debate, they all agreed that people would get to heaven by hearing the gospel and then responding appropriately.

My next question was, "How are people going to hear the gospel?"

Their response: "Through our preaching."

"Fine," I said. "And what will their appropriate response be and how will you know they made that response?"

Answer: "They will pray a prayer to receive God into their hearts."

"Where will this transaction take place?" I asked.

They all liked the idea that it could happen anywhere, but after a little prodding, they admitted that they see most of this happening after a sermon in their church. After getting their responses, I gave them one more opportunity to change or adjust their answers, but they decided to stick with what they had.

We then took a Sanka instant coffee and Vegemite toast break (something I hope never to relive), and when we came back together I summarized their idea of the gospel.

"So let me play back what you said was the reason and the means of planting this church. You are going to start a church so that you can preach the gospel, hope they believe your message, pray a prayer, and go to heaven. Correct?"

They smiled and sheepishly nodded in unison. I pushed a bit more and asked, "What is the gospel?"

Their response: "The message of God's love and forgiveness of our sins and the hope of eternal life."

"So let me keep going," I said. "The gospel is a systematic set of beliefs or doctrines about God, sin, heaven, and hell that you try to get someone to buy into?" Crowd still nodding. "So salvation is viewed as a gift you get when you . . . pray a prayer?" They nodded like a bunch of puppies watching a yoyo. "So a Christian is someone who has prayed a prayer, and a good Christian is someone who has prayed a prayer and consistently comes to your church, gives money, and generally stops doing all the 'biggie' sins." They still nodded. "So a non-Christian, someone who is doomed to hell for eternity, is someone who hasn't . . . prayed the prayer?"

All of a sudden it got a bit quiet. I kept going. "Evangelism, then, must be the process of trying to get someone to pray a prayer. Heaven, this beautiful eternal wildly awesome place, is only for those who have prayed a prayer. And hell, the fire, gnashing of teeth, eternal torment, is for everyone who didn't come to your church, hear your sermon, and pray the prayer?"

By now, I was visibly emotional, as was the wife of one of the church planters. Many of the other leaders were looking down at their feet. Some had put their hands over their faces, and we just sat there quietly.

"I have to be honest." I said after collecting myself. "I would not be interested in coming to your church if that is all you've got going." I was saddened but not surprised, as we have heard the same anemic version of the gospel story for so long here in United States.

Jipped again! The good news is now bad news . . . or no news.

Jesus knew that the only people who would find his news to be bad news would be the people who didn't want to lose control of their lives or "come to the light," as he put it. Everyone else would view his gospel as an attractive alternative to the life they were experiencing. There will always be people who are, at a heart level, completely resistant to Christ. But this book isn't about them. This book is about the millions of people who are openhearted and curious about life and God but who are honestly not finding goodness in the good news that we talk about and that, at times, has been forced down their collective throats.

We have to be honest with ourselves and realize that if the message isn't attractive, and the people of God aren't attractive, then we must not be telling the story right, or we aren't living the story correctly. Maybe we forgot the story, or even worse, maybe no one ever told us the whole story. Maybe you got jipped, too. If so, you may also have jipped others.

Several years ago, I was flying back from San Francisco, and I had one of those "airplane moments" evangelist guys like me have all the time. I was sitting next to a lady who was reading an inspirational book. I asked her what she was reading, and she showed me a collection of positive sayings. She said, "I love these things! They keep me on track and focused on what's most important." I, of course, began to transform from the mild-mannered airplane passenger into *Evangelman*! I was now on the hunt for any chink in her armor (not that she even knew I thought she was wearing armor). I learned that in Youth for Christ: you picture every non-churchgoer as some stoic, rebellious Robocop in inch-thick anti-God armor.

I began by asking her what she thinks is most important in life to her.

"Easy," she said. "My work and my community of friends."

Darn, I thought, *she used the "community" word*. My mind was racing to try to find some angle to expose some area of need, but she began to color in the lines for me.

"I work as a biologist, and I've been specifically working on a cure for AIDS for fourteen years."

"What got you into that line of work?" I asked.

"Many of my friends have died of this disease, and I'm infected myself." I just nodded and listened to her talk about her community. "Everyone I work with is like family. Almost all of us share a real passion for our purpose together, and we even take time every day to gather together, join hands and pray to our benevolent God for his help in finding a cure. They're both my co-laborers and my spiritual family. If all I had was them, that's all I will ever need."

At that point I remembered that in their book, *Lost in America*, Tom Clegg and Warren Bird said that people on Earth have three fundamental needs.[2] They are *transcendence* (the need to connect with the Creator), *significance* (the need to have a purpose in life and do something meaningful), and *community* (the need to connect with others through deeply satisfying relationships). *Hmmm*, I thought, *this gal doesn't appear to have many chinks in her armor. She actually seems pretty darn content*—seems to have transcendence, significance, and community.

For the first time in my life, I felt I didn't have anything to offer. And her description about her holistic missional community sounded like what I'd read in Acts about the early church community.

As we got off the plane, I felt a hand on my shoulder. It was this dear lady. She said, "I'm sorry, I never asked you what you did for work."

"I'm a pastor," I said.

She asked, "What type of church?"

"Oh," I said, "just your average Christian church."

What happened next will always be deeply embedded in my mind. She gently reached down, grabbed both my hands, looked me right in my eyes, and said, "Oh, I'm sure that must be hard to do. I've never found anything attractive about any church or Christians I've ever met. I will pray for you." And then she recited some Celtic blessing over me that sounded like it came straight from the very mouth of Saint Patrick.

She left, and I just stood there babbling to myself. I had just been blessed by some woman who genuinely felt sorry for me because she perceived me to be the poor, searching one. She literally had no chinks. I apparently had a few. Now, deep down, I knew I had something for her. . . . I just wasn't sure what! Or how to bridge this chasm of perception and reality.

Christianity, to her, would probably never be an inspiring path to consider.

I would have dismissed this experience as unique or strange and ultimately put the blame on her for not wanting to know the real God, but I've heard this type of response so many times that I'm left with this reality: the gospel—that is, the huge, life-reorienting story that has had such massive drawing power to just about any spiritual seeker over the centuries—has been reduced to a pathetically simple, doctrinal Podcast that no one is interested in.

Not even me.

The Gospel of God's Kingdom

If our gospel is what people think it is, it's no wonder that it's not worth adding church to a busy recreational weekend.

Yes, people are closed to *our* version of the gospel, but maybe they'd be open to *God's* gospel. God's gospel was and is his way of explaining the whole story. The gospel tells us why we fight with each other, why we have war, pain, suffering, and death. The gospel of Jesus shows the heart of God for humanity and the depths of his love and acceptance and vision for every human being. It gives us hope in the face of injustice, hunger, and poverty, and for recovery from every vice or societal ill. It advocates for community, acceptance, fairness, forgiveness, and love of all people regardless of past mistakes, sexual orientation, or political bias. The Gospel of God's Kingdom helps explain where meaning comes from and how we are to live an integrated experience in light of God's love for his created humanity.

It was this gospel that Jesus knew would be good news to those trying to answer the eternity issue and even the more temporal problems. It was the gospel that Jesus knew would draw people naturally like sheep to a clear-water well. It was good news! Always, in all times, with any person, for one major reason we've lost sight of: the gospel meant that life *now* could be different!

In Adullam, we do an event called a "Big Table" about every eight weeks. We do this because some of our "villages" (our incarnational communities) like to use Sunday morning to serve people in the city. The leader of one of these villages told me that during a "leaf-raking" experience, one of the neighbors they were serving had asked a good question.

"Who are you guys, and why are you doing this?"

Vic, one of our men, answered, "We wanted to do something useful on Sunday morning instead of just going to church."

Now don't overreact to this. Going to meet with God's people to worship is not useless. What Vic was saying is that most people outside church (and many inside) want a larger experience of the gospel. We're all thrilled that the gospel brings great hope and solace about the afterlife, but maybe we're all finding our PostMod side that also wants to see some heaven here and now.

In Genesis 12:2, God's fundamental framework for "blessing" is described. God tells Abram, "I will make you into a great nation and I will bless you; I will make your name great, and you will be a blessing." Now, *blessing*, as we have said, means the "life of God flowing tangibly onto his people." To a Jewish person in the Old Testament, blessing was perceived to be given for this present life. And if it was to reach beyond this life, it was for our children and then their children's children. That is, if God blessed his people, the people would feel and see God now, on this side of eternity. When God gave the Ten Commandments in Deuteronomy 5, he implored his people to obey them "so that it will go well with you" (Deut. 6:18). It was understood that if they lived according to God's ways, they would be happier than if they didn't.

There's a clear connection between the Old Testament concept of "blessing" and Jesus' concept of "the Kingdom of God" described in Mark 1:15. When Jesus came proclaiming the "good news of the Kingdom," or what we would call the "gospel," he was not trying to get people to simply pray a prayer so they could go to heaven. He was saying that anyone can live differently because "my Kingdom is *now*."

When we focus on the gospel primarily as another world to come after we die, we are missing a massive part of the story. We're missing the part that is good news to a real person. The afterlife is an important part of the story and is good news when you're dying, or have a friend who has just passed, or if you happen to be under great persecution and can't even think beyond your prison cell. But when people aren't in close proximity to death, they need to see the difference that God's world makes in their world.

I'm not disputing that our eternal condition is the most important issue, nor am I saying that when the Kingdom shows up in real life that it makes everything rosy. For sure, this latter idea is more attuned to the prosperity doctrines which communicate to people that all God wants to do is bless them so they get everything they want. With the evil that exists in our hearts and in our world, it will always be difficult to enjoy a purely blissful existence on this side of eternity, but that doesn't mean we should reduce a much larger story of God's Kingdom to a simple formula for getting someone into heaven.

In explaining why he came, Jesus in Luke 4:18–19 quotes Isaiah 61:1–2: "The spirit of the Lord is on me, because he has anointed me to preach good news to the poor. He has sent me to proclaim freedom for the prisoners and recovery of sight for the blind, to release the oppressed, to proclaim the year of the Lord's favor." People who heard this in the time of Jesus would have jumped for joy, because it meant some hope for new life now.

In *The Divine Conspiracy*, Dallas Willard paraphrases Jesus' remarkable claim in Mark 1:15 this way: "All the preliminaries have been taken care of," he said, "and the rule of God is now accessible to everyone. Review your plans for living and base your life on this remarkably new opportunity."[3]

Jesus is saying that there is a new Kingdom now, one that's totally different from the kingdom you're accustomed to, and anyone can get in on it. Different things can and should happen now. His message wasn't about just some future blessing of heaven; it was an announcement that his heavenly ways are available in some way here on Earth. Not in fullness, for it will never be heaven here. But you *can have* a slice of heaven here on Earth.

What was the gospel? What is the gospel?

It is the tangible life of God flowing into every nook and cranny of our everyday life. No, blessing doesn't mean our financial "cups running over" or the absence of disease or pain. But it does mean that the "other-world" life does make a tangible difference that can be felt in this life. And when this other-world life shows up, even in the smallest form, it is attractive, and people unconsciously move toward it like thirsty horses stumbling toward a watering hole.

When a father who has been struggling with anger and who verbally rips a hole in the heart of his wife or kids begins to let Christ and his Kingdom win out over his own heart, the family should notice a difference. When that materialistic businessman meets Christ and starts to reinvest his treasures for the benefit of others, there will be an observable difference in the lives of people who receive help and on the face of the man who now knows the joy of giving. When someone adopts a child, brings a kind word of encouragement to someone in jail, renovates a dilapidated home in the inner city, mentors a struggling student, plants trees in an ugly city block, plays music for the elderly, or throws a party for friends ... it's all Kingdom, and it's always good news!

Our culture is starving for something, but this something has to be *massive*. It has to be a challenge, it has to be scary, and it has to be life encompassing for people to even notice.

Are they skeptical? Yes.

Are they jaded? Yes.

Have they lost their appetite? *No!*

We need to be honest about our lame, half-baked message and our even lamer attempts to dress up it up and make it look sexier than it is. My sense is that we'd do better to admit we haven't fully discovered the depths of this story and simply invite people to start digging for it with us again.

In Adullam, during our membership process, I make it a point to ask people not to be "evangelistic." I tell them that I don't want them to try to figure out how to share the gospel with strangers. Sometimes I get a funny look. Instead, I ask them to open up their hearts to a much larger view of life, at which point we talk about the Kingdom. I do ask people to live out and try their hand at Kingdom life, and I tell them that if they live out Kingdom life, they will have plenty of opportunities to share different aspects of Christ with people. The difference is that instead of having to pursue people, people will be drawn toward them with curiosity and openness.

At this point, you may be thinking, "All well and good, but shouldn't you have at least told the lady on the plane that she was still missing God and will spend eternity in hell unless she gets her act together?"

I believe it does more harm than good when we start with our stripped down, minimalized version of such a grand mystery. I think we should start by looking for ways to witness to this gospel by bringing tangible slices of heaven down to life on Earth, and continue to do this until those we're reaching out to acknowledge that our ways are "good news" to them. If you're truly living the good news, you'll have plenty of opportunities to explain the theological aspects of the gospel. But if we continue to lead off with words about the gospel instead of acts of the gospel, we'll continue to jip people.

Reflection

o In what ways have you felt jipped by a short-sheeted gospel?

o

10

ANOTHER ANGLE

IT'S NOT UNCOMMON, after enlarging one's view of the gospel, to feel discombobulated and confused about how to move forward. It's like a skier who gets lost in the woods for five days without food and, after being found, is taken to a high-end buffet. He is salivating and desperate to dive in, but he stands there dazed because he's not sure where to start.

Often people say to us, "Okay, I'm getting the point. You keep pushing for the ancient/incarnational way to reemerge and offer an alternative to the attractional paradigm of church and the small gospel, but how does it really play out? How does the conversion process actually happen? How is it different than what we are doing now?"

Let's look first at the attractional approach and then compare it to the incarnational approach.

The Attractional Approach

When we say "attractional approach," we're talking about the attempt to draw to church, people with whom we have no relationship. Through program, presentation, or preaching, we hope that people will choose to "come to us." The challenge of this approach has nothing to do with our main Sunday service. We don't think it's wrong to have a big church service or do corporate worship and teaching well. What we critique here is the pathway that we create for people's entrance into church and the subsequent pathway for discipleship.

You'll notice that in an "attractional church," the process usually begins when we invite someone to church to hear a sermon. Without going any further, you can already see that the process breaks down, simply because people won't be coming to church only for that reason.

However, for the sake of the illustration, let's assume that we get lucky, and a few folks happen to show up. A sermon is preached, and the pastor likely gives an invitation to make a decision for Christ. If the person has been looking for God and is drawn in by the message, then the person may confess belief. That is to say, they've been touched by the sermon, they are moved at the heart level, and they therefore sign up with God. To do this, often they repeat a prayer that closes the deal.

After the person has become a Christian (prayed the prayer), we invite them to join our church, at which point we begin cognitive discipleship. We help them learn more about Christ, their decision, the scriptures, and the general 101 of Christianity (prayer, Bible, church, and so on). Because our focus in this mode is to "get someone saved," we tend to measure our success by counting confessions.

This systematic, linear, attractional flow unintentionally communicates to people that there is a clear line of who's in and who's out, based on a moment of belief. We also communicate that you can't really belong with us unless you believe what we believe. In other words, belief enables belonging.

Let me recognize that most of you reading this book probably came to faith in this model, as I did. We were probably brought to church by our families, and thus we heard God's Word, we believed and prayed a genuine prayer of repentance and confession. For many of you, this was a day you remember, and we should all be thankful that our pathway to God was so clean.

At the same time, we have to remember that it worked because the dominant culture that surrounded the church was not that different from the people inside the church. People outside the faith generally had a God orientation, the church was at the center of American life and thought, and you could still get people to come simply because they thought that was where all the God stuff happens. This continues to be a somewhat fruitful process whenever you're dealing with those who grew up in church or who were on the fringes. They will tend still to go back to church when looking for help from God.

The Incarnational Approach

Although the attractional approach will continue to be influential with people who have some context for church, we must accept that the growing post-everything culture must be wooed through a more incarnational process. In other words, the greater the cultural distance from organized religion a person is, the greater the need for an incarnational presence of a gospel community.

Table 10.1 may help you see some of the differences. This presentation is greatly simplified, but we hope it provides a helpful way to contrast the two approaches.

You'll notice quickly that in opposition to an attractional process that focuses on creating a place where people can go to and hear the message of the gospel, the incarnational approach tries to first create a people to which someone can *belong so that they can feel or see aspects of the gospel lived out*. Remember, this community of belonging is where the Discovery Zone (discussed in Chapter Nine) begins. As we'll show in later chapters, the options for these belonging environments can be just about anywhere, thus giving people a much wider range of options for starting their faith journey.

The next step involves the Sojourner *confessing interest*, not belief. This may not sound as exciting, but as you develop eyes to see their interest you will easily see God in their curiosity and their genuine interest in you and your community. The proof of their interest will be seen as they begin to initiate meaningful conversations about their life. They'll ask you more about your life. They'll invite you deeper into their lives, the lives of their children, and you'll be invited to enter the world of their friends. These are all evidence that God is on the move in their hearts.

Table 10.1. Comparison of Attractional and Incarnational Approaches.

Attractional Approach	Incarnational Approach
Unbeliever is invited to church	Sojourner is invited to belong
Unbeliever confesses belief	Sojourner confesses interest
Unbeliever repeats a prayer	Sojourner experiences the good news
Believer joins church	Sojourner participates in community
Cognitive discipleship	Experiential apprenticeship
Focus: Counting confessions	Focus: Transformation
Believing enables belonging	Belonging enables believing

Remember, the conversion process isn't just about people hearing the truth; it's about people being ready to receive the truth. So our posture—the nonverbals that we give off that let people know they're loved, that we care enough to listen or even wait—are just as important as our spoken message.

In Adullam, we encourage all of our people to avoid making any formal invitation to anything until someone has initiated a few of the fore-mentioned interests. If they continue to invite themselves toward us and our community, then finally we do call them to our community.

After more than a year, my neighbor Steve came over and asked me why all the cars were in front of our home on Saturday morning. I said, "It's Matt, Rich, Tim, and a bunch of other guys you've met. We're having a men's breakfast where we talk about God and life. You're more than welcome to join us." He did. The important element wasn't that I invited Steve, but that Steve had become friends with me and most of the guys in this community long before he invited himself toward us. He was showing me that he was *interested* in us.

As people confess interest, it means they are starting to belong with us. The next thing that begins to happen is they begin to *experience the good news*, even before they know what it is.

During a Saint Paddy's Day celebration, we had a very mixed group of struggling saints, curious Sojourners, and a few happy pagans. We were enjoying a great evening together, and to close the time, I invited them all into the main room. I handed out little pieces of paper that had Celtic blessings on them. Some were funny and some were authentic blessings. Some were even scripture. I gave them a quick word on why the Irish enjoyed blessing each other and then let everyone read theirs to the group. As we went around, I noticed that some people who didn't initially feel comfortable joining us did come in to participate. As the blessings were read, people got quiet, some put down their drinks, and it was obvious that everyone was picking up on something good. As people left, many whom I barely knew hugged me and thanked me for providing such a meaningful night for them and their friends.

Whether it's receiving a verbal blessing, getting to watch people love each other, enjoying a warm peaceful house, or having someone sit down to listen to you, the good news should be felt before it's explained.

Simultaneously, or at least quite soon afterward, the next process begins. The Sojourner begins to *participate in the community* of Christ followers. They start inviting people to their houses, they participate in benevolent actions of the community, and they participate more in the spiritual dialogue and life of the missional people.

A young girl named Mel came into one of our communities and learned that some of our folks were taking a trip to New Orleans to continue a project we'd been working on for about a year. She signed up without knowing who was going, so my wife, Cheryl, and one of her village girls named Laura went along so that Mel wouldn't feel strange. I met with Mel after the trip, and she said, "I'm learning that Jesus really changes everything!" She went on to express that she wants to use some of her contacts and passions to continue working with people in need. She spoke as if she is getting some clarity on the purpose of her life. For Mel, participation in the community was a natural reality, not a hope. Mel doesn't have to be taught that Christians help the world; she got to experience what Christians do.

The beauty of this part of the process is that the Sojourners are being discipled or apprenticed in the way of the Christ followers. We use the word *apprentice* because it's more accurate to the intent of what Jesus meant by his use of the word *disciple*.

For example, as I've tried to survive ministry and church planting, my "tent-trade" has been that of a house painter. If I wanted to disciple you in the classic evangelical or attractional church way, I would say, "Okay, today we're painting Tom's house. I want you to sit on the tailgate of truck and watch me paint it." As you did this, you would learn quite a bit. You'd see how I tape off the windows, how I spray the siding and pull off the tape after I'm done. In some sense, you'd have a general idea of what a painter does, and you'd be able to describe to someone the basics of what a house painter does.

However, if I wanted to *apprentice* you in being a house painter, then I would call you off the tailgate. I'd hand you the tape gun and tape and make you do a window. Then I'd give you the control of the paint sprayer and help you up onto the ladder. I'd teach you everything you need to know about every aspect of doing a paint job, because my motives are different. I would only apprentice someone whom I was going to depend on to do what I did. My goal is to make you a painter, not just someone who can talk about painting.

How many pastors have pulled their hair out trying to "make a disciple" *after* someone comes to faith? With the incarnational approach, you don't have to worry about it. It happens naturally.

I know that some of you are asking, "Where's the Bible in all of this community stuff?" The answer is, Everywhere! It's in my car, so that when my friend has a question I can show him what I mean. It comes across in my e-mails as I respond to people's questions. It's in the middle of our community gatherings. It's in the homes of my unbelieving friends, because as soon as they express curiosity, I buy them a Bible and ask them to begin to read so we can talk more. It's active, present at all times. As opposed to counting confessions of faith or tracking church attendance to know if we're making an impact, in the incarnational process, we celebrate every moment of *transformation*. We watch relationships move deeper into the community, we look for greater openness in conversations, we relish good evenings of fun and deep dialogue. We note people's change in behavior and their wide open hearts while we talk through the scriptures. We celebrate their personal participation in how we live and whom we help. In other words, we track the change in their lives, not some prayer that they may pray. Even though a baptism feels like a culminating event, it's just one moment in a long string of mystical movements toward Christ. At a structural or leadership level, we do monitor how many villages—those places of belonging—are available, and how people are moving deeper into them. More on that in the next chapter.

The incarnational way culminates in this primary difference: *Belonging enables believing*. So often when people ponder this alternative they come alive with excitement. Here are some common responses we hear about the incarnational way.

- ○ It takes the pressure off. My job is to provide a place of belonging, not push the Bible on people.
- ○ I can trust God to do the "converting" thing.
- ○ As an introvert and a person with hospitality gifts, I now know I can be a major part of the evangelistic process by creating belonging environments.
- ○ It puts the focus back on my inner life instead of what I say or don't say to people.
- ○ I have to become good news to my family and friends if I want to influence them.
- ○ This fits the natural flow of my life. We're so busy, but what you've said is that everywhere I am and any person I touch consistently is someone that God will use me to help reach. I don't have to add anything to my schedule; I just have to be intentional and authentic in the places I find myself in.

In this incarnational model, everything hinges on having a people or a community to invite people to belong to. Community is the center of the entire missional incarnational approach.

I have enjoyed all the relational and friendship evangelism books I've read over the years, but there's a glaring hole in both those approaches. They suggest that you try to woo people alone. When you try to do

evangelism by yourself, your only option for continued spiritual movement is to get people to church. We find people who have developed great
relationships with people at their office, their Starbucks, or wherever, but
it always seems to dead-end. "I can't get them to come to church!"

The issue is not you. The issue is that you don't have a community in
which they can find belonging.

○

_____

Reflection

○ Describe some of the benefits of the incarnational approach for
   you and your community.

○ What is getting in the way of you providing the incarnational path
   for others?

_____

○

11

LIFT UP THE HOOD

WHEN WAS THE LAST TIME you lifted the hood of your car? Probably a long time ago. With today's computerized engines and all that new electronic stuff, who can understand what's going on in there anyway? The real issue is whether or not the dumb thing runs, right?

Wrong—for cars and for churches.

The incarnational approach to church sounds free-flowing and natural, but it requires some organization and structure to propel it forward. We have hesitated to talk about the structure of church because we understand that it brings up a lot of emotion, both positive and negative.

Wherever we have people, and vision, and a common call (especially if that call is from God), we have to commit at some level to structures, even if we're helping coach the neighborhood soccer team.

Most of the young leaders and church planters we work with love the incarnational approach. They can't wait to get out of the office, get more relational, and provide a natural environment where people can muse together.

To help inch them forward, we ask one question: "What happens if it works?"

"Huh?" they often grunt. "What do you mean?"

"You know, what if all your spontaneous, natural, relational, nonreligious ways affect someone's heart and they want to join in? And what happens if that keeps working the same way for hundreds of people?"

The common response: "I don't know."

Well, we think we should know. We think that's what the organism of the church is all about. I say *organism* because an organism is natural, and many of its functions happen without prompting or control, but whether it's the human body, a plant, or even a jellyfish, there are structures that allow for its movement, growth, and protection. It's the same in God's natural movement of the church.

Whether it be mega-church, cell church, house church, simple church, or hybrid church, structures can either hinder mission and the incarnational presence of the gospel or free up the gospel toward a cohesive movement of people. As we'll see, any form or size of church can be attractional or incarnational.

In this chapter and in Chapter Twelve, we look at both sides. Let's start with a structure that has limited the gospel movement.

The Pyramid

Figure 11.1 represents the general structure of how church has been done in the United States for quite a while. It is a pyramid, with pastors at the top, staff and lay leaders in the middle, and the congregation at the base. We got this pyramid from Constantine. Just another Christendom hangover. There are a few key things to notice about it.

First, the leadership or pastoral hierarchy exists to serve the needs and wants of the congregation. Pastors and leaders are hired to maintain the functions of the church (teaching, administration, sacraments, and vision). That is, they are expected to personally do, or get others to do, things that keep the structure alive. This paradigm of leadership is why the average church in America tends to be about seventy people. That is the number of people that one individual can do all these things for. If there is church staff below the pastor, their primary job is to serve the pastor or to act as liaisons between the head pastor and the congregation.

Second, the congregational members, by and large, are fairly inactive and are not ultimately responsible for making a tangible difference in culture. One church I worked with had as its assimilation process the strategy of making every new person take a six-month tour of duty as a greeter in the church foyer. As I got to meet some of the greeters, I met a man who was the president of a Fortune 15 company, a woman who was a world-class artist, and a head coach for an NCAA

Figure 11.1   The Traditional-Attractional Church Model.

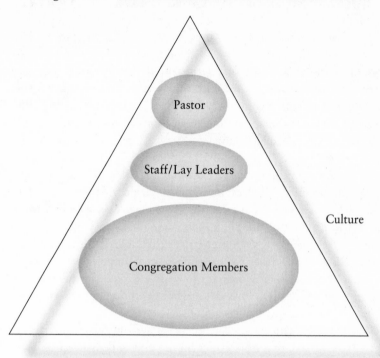

Pastor

Staff/Lay Leaders

Culture

Congregation Members

Source: Adapted from Hunsberger, G. R., and Van
Gelder, C. *The Church Between Gospel and Culture:
The Emerging Mission in North America.* Grand
Rapids, Mich.: Eerdmans, 1996, p. 329.

football team. These three people alone represented incredible gifts and
leadership abilities but were "mobilized" to shake hands, smile, and give
out brochures.

In more contemporary churches, the pyramid is often inverted, because
the pastor and their pastoral team usually see their jobs as equipping the
congregation to do the work both inside the church and out in the world.
The contemporary model usually grows larger, primarily because it tends
to do a better job of creating momentum or movement among its people.
It also tends to provide a better Sunday presentation and programs that
draw more people.

The problem, however, is that most of the real growth in such churches
comes from other churches (or from those individuals who have "tapped
out" for a few years and are looking to return). Because of the expertise of

the pastor and the excellence of the programs, the average congregational member remains relatively consumer oriented and inactive in the world and the unchurched culture remains . . . unchurched.

When we look at the traditional-attractional church structure in light of the incarnational model we've been discussing, it's clear that the attractional model falls short. It doesn't provide a place of *discovery* where truth can be seen or felt and where can people observe the benefits of Kingdom life being lived out in the context of community. There may be some discovery in a worship moment, or as people look around to see others smiling, but it's hard to unpack a new Kingdom experience in a 50-minute service.

It's also difficult to find *inclusive community* in this structure, or any level of real community, if by *community* we mean something more than knowing each other's name or shaking hands by the espresso cart in the church foyer, it's not here. Sojourners are nowhere around us in this model, and real community is replaced by Christian affinity groups at best.

Where in this model could Sojourners see us bringing deep meaning through sacrifice and risk? Where do they pick up on our real *values*? It's pretty hard to pick up on the values of a revolutionary movement of people inside the church walls.

How many people can *model* the Kingdom way in this structure? At best, the pastor can share a story about his life during the week that gives people a glimpse into active faith. But you still have only one person modeling instead of an entire movement of people living out their own Tangible Kingdom for people to experience.

In Adullam, we've made the deliberate decision not to be very excellent or polished during our main gathering, simply because we don't want to create an environment that is so good that it causes people to feel positioned as observers. Because I want myself and our people to have time to be incarnational in the world, we don't take up their time working on the church service. We don't have a worship practice, and I spend only a few hours a week planning our time together, which includes sermon preparation. Sometimes, we even cancel our gathering so people can do something alternative to a worship gathering. If we say that the "big thing" isn't the "main thing," then we must reflect that in how we spend our time.

There's a great leadership principle I heard once: "What you give leadership to will always grow." That is, if I give my time to getting in shape, I'll get in shape. If I give my time to my business, my business will grow. If I give my time to creating a great teaching ministry on Sunday morning, then we'll provide a service to people who really like that kind of ministry.

Since we know that most Sojourners don't wake up Sunday morning looking for a good sermon, we've decided to put our energy, efforts, and focus into the incarnational aspects of our church instead of the presentational aspects. As such, we double the number of villages each year, and I get to enjoy not being pressured to be that good on Sunday. I don't need to hit a sermonic triple or a home run; I just need a bloop single with an occasional gapper to keep us moving.

I once made an inaccurate theological statement on Palm Sunday. I said that Jesus' legs were broken by the Roman guards. Right as the words came fumbling out of my mouth, I tried to catch them in midair and reel them in, but my worship leader beat me to it and said, "Uh, Hugh, actually, they didn't." I was caught in a moment that clearly exposed that I had only an hour of sleep the previous night due to my son's epilepsy. I misspoke a simple statement that I had done a paper on in seminary and that even my kids knew.

In many churches, I'd have been fired before the next Sunday for incompetence. In my church, we all just laughed and made the correction as a community and moved on. During the subsequent weeks, several new couples called me to tell me how they were refreshed by the community's openness to let the pastor make a blunder without expecting perfection. Was I surprised and embarrassed by this public faux pas? Yes. Would I want this to happen again? Never. But it did illustrate the point that Sojourners, spiritually disoriented God seekers, and jaded Christians aren't looking for the best stage presence or programs, but they will stay committed to real people and a mission that makes sense in the real world.

The attractional church structure gauges success by how many people show up on Sunday and the all-too-few stories of people committing their lives to God. But we don't know whether disciples or apprentices of Christ are being made or whether we're making a tangible difference in the culture that we're called to reach.

The point of this discussion is not to judge this traditional church structure, to call it bad or out of date. We simply want to show that this structure of *attractional* church makes it very hard to communicate, show, or create a place of belonging where the whole gospel can be *discovered*. It's not a matter of the heart; it's simply that the structure limits missionality and the ability to be incarnational as a community.

Meaningful mission needs some structure, some framework on which to build God's community. In Chapter Twelve, we look at some new structures (actually, they're ancient structures) that make sense.

○
_____

Reflection

Okay, take a break. We realize what we just said can be a real bummer. Instead of overreflecting on the past, let's quickly move to some good news, some solid hope for a new structure that will deliver the goods of the gospel.

_____
○

12

TIP IT OVER

A FEW YEARS AGO I decided to live out a dream I've had since my early teens. Some people have dreams of climbing Mt. Everest, running a marathon, or seeing all seven wonders of the world. Mine was simpler. I just wanted to own a Jeep. Cheryl wanted a Subaru Outback. You know, something *functional*, as she put it. I said, "Honey, fun is also a function of life." She didn't buy it, but I did . . . go out and buy it. Blue, soft top, with this cute little back hatch. In my excitement, the first summer I took the top off and vowed to leave it off all season. After all, they say that Colorado has only twenty-five days of rain, so I thought I was being quite practical.

On my ride home from the dealership and on many other days since then, I've been caught in one of those Denver 30-minute thundershowers that happen about every day in July and August around 3:00 pm. I'd act like it was fun, or that I wasn't bothered by being pelted with rain, hail, or the occasional white squall that a semi-truck would launch over my roll bar, but I'm sure it was obvious to the other drivers that I was the "impractical guy." Often I've ripped a fingernail off or smashed my fingers trying to wedge both of my daughters' massive hockey bags through the back vinyl window, and I've now counted six times that the communion bread and church supplies have flown out the side windows on the way to our gathering.

I'm learning that form must follow function, but also that we should assess whether or not our original function is the right one. If fun is my primary function, then the Jeep may still work. But if toting hockey bags and being able to talk on the cell phone or getting good gas mileage are my main functions, then the Jeep may not be the right form. I still have the Jeep, but let me move on.

The pyramid structure was an appropriate form when a large portion of the culture valued and looked for a good church to go to—when the leaders were respected by the culture and when people assumed you go to church to find God. The form fit the function. But when the culture is no longer looking for a church to go to, isn't that interested in church music, sermons, or programs, or when they don't innately value or trust church leaders, the functions of church must be adjusted. And thus the form must adjust in kind.

What is the main function? I hope you now agree that the primary function is to actively move into the culture to embody and enflesh the good news into every nook and cranny of this world. The function of the church is to be God's missionary hands to a world that is looking for something tangible to grab onto. If that is the function, then the form must allow for this to happen. This means that the incarnational church must have a new structure.

We believe there is a church structure that may help access and extend the Tangible Kingdom. To see it, we put a crow bar under one corner of the tradition-attractional pyramid shown in Figure 11.1 and tip it over on its side. The result is pictured in Figure 12.1. (*Note:* In some of your settings, dynamite may be required.)

Wait a minute—what happened to the leadership? Where are the church leaders positioned in our tipped-over structure? Out in front, right?

A growing trend among those individuals leaving large attraction model churches is to reconfigure around small church, house church, or no church. When they do so, these individuals often adopt a disdain for the concept of leadership. They like a more flat, everyone-on-the-same-level, no-authority approach. Likewise in the corporate world, you read about companies like Starbucks, Nike, and Google that create a collaborative team environment that inspires people to action based on shared goals and cooperation.

Even though some of these adjustments are natural, we believe that leaders are still very much needed. But their role, positioning, and means of influencing are different.

The scriptures call for people to trust, work with, respect, give to, and even submit to godly leaders. Obviously, these scriptures were not written to Christians who only show up to a weekly church service, but to small communities that lived in close proximity and were structured in a tight relational network. There were few abuses of power because the relational bonds were well established and the commitment to the community was paramount. Church history from Saint Patrick to the Moravians, in addition to Paul, Peter, Titus, and Timothy, has given us healthy pictures of incarnational communities and the posture and practices of leadership. We see great collaboration, shared leadership, teamwork, natural authority, and mutual submission by everyone in the community.

When looking at the need for leadership structures, the question shouldn't begin with "Who should lead?" Or, "How many leaders should there be?" But rather, "How can leaders model an incarnational pathway that others can follow?"

Tipping the church pyramid on its side is a lot like riding around with your pals in your dad's '56 Impala, and just for kicks, slamming on the brakes. You may remember watching all your buddies flying over the front seat and wedging their faces against the front windshield. That's what happens when the pyramid is tipped over. Everyone in the congregation goes flying forward and jams up against the pastor and pastoral staff. We're all in this together, each of us committed to following the lead of the one in front of us.

In Adullam, we had to begin by modeling missional life for about two years. We had no followers, only a bunch of relational connections with disconnected people. We had no authority, no title, and no one even knew we were praying for God to build something out of this diverse group of people. All we had was our life and a pathway people could follow. Cheryl and I took the primary role of allowing our home to be Grand Central Station. We initiated and provided the social and spiritual leadership to ensure that about forty people met each other often while experiencing a deep level of community. Quickly, however, it became obvious that for missionality to continue, we had to slam on the brakes and let some people jam up next to us.

I'm still in front, but I'm not the only one anymore. As the first community grew beyond our ability to keep everyone together under one roof, we had to ask others to live out what they had seen us live out. In incarnational and missional churches, this process of loading up the car and then hitting the brakes must happen consistently. It's a main function of the incarnational structure. The difference is that I'm not leading from above or on top of the community, but from in front and alongside. Am I needed? Yes. If I don't lead, there's no movement, and if I don't get out of the way and let others jump in front, then I'm not leading well. The "missional people" are a key aspect of our structure. They must increase in depth and numbers if missionality is to continue beyond the initial leaders.

Before you jump to the conclusion that a pastor who is not tipping over the pyramid is a "bad" leader, keep in mind that getting back on mission is a *process*. Restructuring leadership is the *hardest thing to do*, even if the heart is willing.

Most pastors we work with would love to lead from the front instead of from above, from the streets instead of from the office. But they don't because so many people still expect them to keep the spiritual vending machine spitting out all the goodies!

The oval of missional people in Figure 12.1 illustrates how everyone has to readjust, not just the pastors, even though the pastors must start the process. They need to model the new way forward, but each Christian must also move toward the front and get accustomed to the

Figure 12.1   The Missional Diagram.

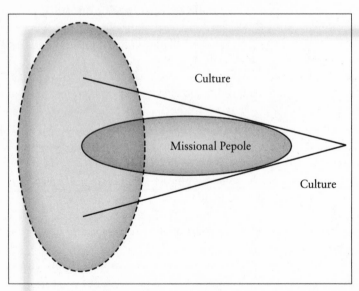

Source: Hunsberger, G. R., and Van Gelder, C. *The Church Between Gospel and Culture: The Emerging Mission in North America.* Grand Rapids, Mich.: Eerdmans, 1996, p. 329.

pastor's new tendency to slam on the brakes. Pastors should provide only what the followers of Christ can't get on their own. Said another way, followers can't expect the pastors to give them what they can provide for themselves. Even more important, followers should expect to give what they can provide to others. No more free rides or back seat drivers; its time to cram a whole lot more people up front!

So, who are the missional people? They are the individuals committed to forming their character and lifestyle after those of Christ and who are compelled to live out their faith in the context of a community.

At least once a week, I get an e-mail from someone who has found our Web site and reads our story. They're usually from people who have burned out on their own church and are searching the Internet for another. The writers usually want to be a part of an "emerging church," as they often put it. Yet after a few months of participating with us, the initial inspiration and intrigue tends to wear off, and their true interest emerges: consumerism.

One couple had been with us for about a month. They had been pastors in Texas, and once they moved to Denver they felt that Adullam had become home. I met with them twice, and it seemed that they really understood the cost and opportunity of being a part of our missional people.

"Take a few months," I suggested. "Get to know some folks, but work even harder at getting to know your neighbors so that you can maybe form a new village made up of mostly Sojourners." A few months went by, and before one of our Sunday gatherings, they came up to me in tears and described how disconnected they felt. As the wife was crying, she said, "This church seems cold and we have had a hard time connecting. We've asked you to help us plug into a village, but you won't help us. In our last church, we had classes where people could connect and you don't have any classes."

In my past attractional church life, I would have put my arms around them, prayed for them, and spent some time the next week trying to find friends for them. This time, and sadly for them, my response was different.

"John and Jill," I said, "this is the wrong place for you. It sounds like you need a church that provides some things for you that we can't." I then redirected them to another church nearby. We have a link on our Web site now that helps people find other churches that offer unique programs and services. How did I know John and Jill weren't a fit with us? The giveaway was that while they were crying about not being connected, we had 150 people standing behind them scarfing down donuts, talking, laughing and . . . connecting. They were the only ones sitting down waiting for the church service to start dispensing worship goodies. They had missed the obvious. We had been having church for 30 minutes!

For the structure to support the ongoing mission, there's no way around the fact that leaders must call people beyond where they've been. They must create new structures that help people move with them and at the same time gently remove consumer-oriented services.

I've discovered that in most cases the church environments we've created for consumers fosters a "softness" that hinders people's growth and involvement in God's mission. This couple had been in paid professional ministry, but they were still expecting someone to "plug them in," start a class for them, or find them some friends.

Dietrich Bonhoeffer spoke of this in his book, *Life Together:* "He who loves his dream of a community more than the Christian community itself becomes a destroyer of the latter, even though his personal intentions may be ever so honest and earnest and sacrificial."[1] Said another way, people who only dream of community usually destroy it, but those who love people without expectation unknowingly create it.

This is why we have a solid line around the "missional people" oval in Figure 12.1. It represents that there are clearly outlined convictions, habits of life, and "rules" for mission that people commit to. We use the word *rules* in the monastic sense. Rules represent the habits of life that the community desires that everyone in the community live out proactively. The Benedictine Rules include "prayer and work." Cyrenian Orders, based on Simon the Cyrene, live around the call of "sharing the burden" and tend to focus on the burdens of the homeless. Trappist Monks commit to "solitude, silence in prayer, work, and a disciplined life." Contemporary neomonastic faith communities like "Small Boat, Big Sea" in Sydney, Australia, have weekly rhythms around "blessing, eating, listening, and learning."

Neomonastic Church

Not everyone can be expected to live according to the rules of a cloistered monastic life, nor is this book advocating that level of commitment, but we can encourage and create structures that help everyone intentionalize specific habits that help us go further. In doing so, we must risk offending some in the hopes of charting out a new type of inspiring Christian story.

In a world that has lost respect for the Christian movement, we suggest that each faith community and each church find its "neomonastic" rules of life and mission. It's the job of leadership to model, clearly articulate, and provide structures that motivate and encourage these habits while at the same time limiting or filtering out those individuals who don't want to be involved. Hebrews 10:24—"And let us consider how we may spur one another on towards love and good deeds"—is not just a call from the pulpit for consumer Christians to make sure to tithe and have their daily devotions. It represents how the early faith communities created environments of grace-filled expectations, where the leaders modeled and expected the Kingdom to show up, and organized their people in ways that would foster their countercultural missional mandate.

When Christians from other contexts come to visit Adullam, I usually take them out for coffee after their second visit. I have to do this in order to be sure they understand what they're getting into. Just as Christians are coming to check us out, I also check them out. In many cases, I intentionally try to surface any consumer tendencies that may hurt them, or us, down the road. I speak boldly about Adullam, not as a church, but as a mission, and explain that if they come with us, they'll have to get on mission. I tell them our story so they see how we live and how God forms us from our habits, and then I articulate what we hope they will share with others.

I show them the diagram that appears as Figure 12.2 and point out the little specks in the space between the missional people oval and the larger Sojourner oval.

I usually ask them, "What do you think these dots mean?" Then I make sure they know that to us, the dots represent people who want to call themselves Christ followers without tangibly following him into mission. They're "pew sitters," people who know a lot of Bible verses, who like to be plugged in and go to classes. They have bucketloads of ministry ideas and love to lead from the top and share their ideas from the top, but they really don't want to live the life of a missional person, sacrificing in order to provide an inclusive community for others. In other words, they are people who only want to experience community if it benefits them.

We usually have about a 50/50 ratio of individuals who leave after that first talk and those who go with us. Although we could grow the church faster if I let pew sitters enjoy our main gathering, we are committed to being faithful to this mission, and therefore we are more concerned about who is with us on mission rather than how many people show up on Sunday.

Perhaps you're feeling this approach is a bit harsh. Maybe you think leaders don't have the right to do this. Quite possibly you believe a church should try to serve anyone with any needs, at every level of spiritual maturity.

It's really not a matter of whether or not church leaders should meet the needs of everyone in the church, or whether or not you're called to

Figure 12.2   Pew Sitters in the Missional Diagram.

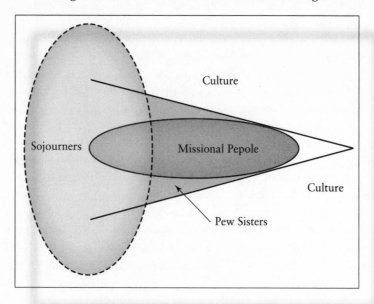

Source: Hunsberger, G. R., and Van Gelder, C. *The*
Church Between Gospel and Culture: The Emerging
Mission in North America. Grand Rapids, Mich.:
Eerdmans, 1996.

provide all things for all people. Each church should hear the call from God as to what they are or aren't to be about. Each pastor or pastoral team needs to adjust the structures to fit their collective call.

Something Christians easily miss is how many times Jesus limits who will be able to follow him. To those asking if they can go with him, he intentionally said things he knew would cause them to cramp up and head for cover. Things like:

> "Whoever eats my flesh and drinks my blood has eternal life" (John 6:54). *See ya!*

> Oh, your dad is dead: "Let the dead bury their own dead" (Luke 9:59–60). *Sheesh! You're mean, man!*

> "The Son of Man has no place to lay his head" (Luke 9:58). *Follow you? . . . No way!*

After a bunch of followers turned and walked away, Jesus asked his disciples, "You do not want to leave too, do you?" (John 6:67). How are we to interpret this? How does the way of Jesus line up with the way of our consumer-oriented churches that try to make sure there's enough parking for everyone? Does there need to be incredible discernment and grace alongside our church practices? Of course. Even in my coffee-talk with Adullam visitors, I wait to drop the bomb until I've heard their story. If they're struggling in faith, have no faith, or have been hurt in church, then I'm as cordial and encouraging as Mr. Rogers. But if I discern they have been walking with God a long time, have put in a few thousand hours in church, seem overly religious or more interested in lofty theological debate than in rolling up their shirt sleeves to serve, I get a little more assertive. Before God, I have to protect the communal and missional calling of our people.

I advise you not to be afraid of moving in this direction. Most of you have experienced monastic life at some level. If you've been in the military or on an athletic team, or worked for a small company, grew up in a tight extended family, or had a club that you started in first grade, you remember the benefits of stating your purpose and filtering out people who weren't willing to play by your rules, and you experienced a close sense of community because of it.

You may ask, "Doesn't this approach lead to legalism that might cause people to hate church again? Won't people think you're forcing them into behavior?" "Won't you lose the great value of 'grace' that allows people to be themselves without feeling like they have to commit to the 'works' of a church?"

We don't think so. The habits, rules, rhythms, and convictions of a community that is bent on God's mission will be so positive and spiritually formative that they could never be conceived as a "have to" . . . but rather a "get to." The legalism that has stripped some segments of the church of its heart, causing people to lose interest, has been based on pharisaical values of head knowledge and separation from the world. The convictions we need to rally around should be about life giving, community transformation, holistic personal growth, sacrifice, beauty, blessing, and world renewal. Who wouldn't want to be a part of a people committed to something that brings personal meaning and makes the world a better place?

A documentary about Ernest Shackleton's early twentieth-century exposition to the South Pole shows the classified ad Shackleton put in a London newspaper:

"Men wanted for hazardous journey, small wages, bitter cold, long months of complete darkness, constant danger, safe return doubtful. Honor and recognition in case of success." Ernest Shackleton.[2]

Men responded to Shackleton's advertisement in droves. Why? Because the mission was clear. The cost and potential loss both drew the right men and made sure the wrong men didn't sign up. God's mission, similarly, is not for the faint of heart. Even becoming a Christian, according to Jesus, should be weighed heavily. Luke says, "Suppose one of you wants to build a tower. Will he not first sit down and estimate the cost to see if he has enough money to complete it? For if he lays the foundation and is not able to finish it, everyone who sees it will ridicule him, saying, 'This fellow began to build and was not able to finish'" (Luke 14:28–30).

Although Adullam looks like a church from the outside, we're straining to strengthen our neomonastic call. This means that our "gathering"—or what people used to call "church"—is an aspect of what we do, but not the only thing. The gathering is where we . . . gather. That's it. It's a place that anyone can come to and not feel any pressure at any level. Grace flows heavy over immaturity, consumerism, morality, and immorality (sometimes even legalism). But as people stay with us and move more deeply into our life, they are confronted with our communal calling. And the mission is what compels us to challenge, confront, and occasionally reposition people away from us in order to maintain the "rules" of our "order and calling."

Welcoming Sojourners

In Figure 12.3, you'll notice that the pyramid lost its bottom end when it tipped over. There's no closed loop or limit to entrance into this mission. The big oval that extends to the left beyond the triangle is also included inside the congregation and is labeled "Sojourners," meaning "temporary, spiritually curious but disoriented God seekers." When I talked about people showing curiosity toward the community, I was talking about Sojourners. They will either travel relationally with us or move away from us.

The dotted line around the Sojourner oval is very important. Unlike the missional people, Sojourners can come and go as they like. They can sin, cuss, swear at their kids, yell at the ref, spend their money on useless endeavors, vote any way they want, chew tobacco, and hold any sexual orientation they like, all without judgment or pressure.

When we spoke of having an inclusive Christian community that welcomes Sojourners, this is what we meant. Such folks can travel with us and our congregation without complete buy-in to the faith or change in lifestyle. In fact, the reason we want them with us is so that we can help them—on their own timetable—come to faith. As much as the missional people need some clear rails to run on (or "rules of life"), the Sojourners

Figure 12.3   Sojourners in the Missional Diagram.

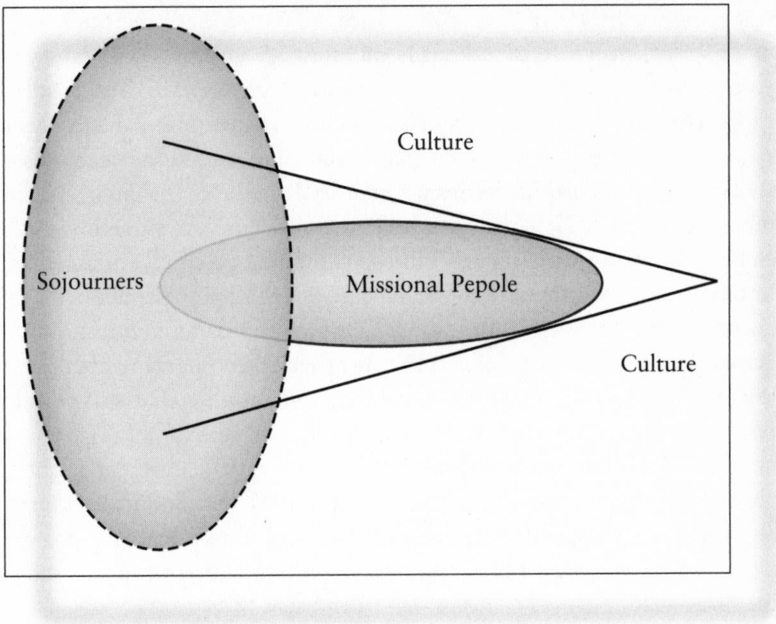

Source: Hunsberger, G. R., and Van Gelder, C. *The Church Between Gospel and Culture: The Emerging Mission in North America*. Grand Rapids, Mich.: Eerdmans, 1996.

need only an environment in which they can be eyewitnesses to our life without feeling any pressure to be like us.

In our first church in Portland, our worship leader and many of our key musicians were extremely well respected in the city and night club scene. When not in church, they were playing in public venues. This was part of their lifestyle. Our missional people knew that I wanted them to invite their unchurched musician friends to join us in the worship experience. And yes, also to play on Sunday.

I received enough e-mails over this to know that some people perceive the church to be sacred space cleansed from all pagan participation. I'm not sure where we got this from, since God told us he doesn't actually live in temples made with human hands. But there apparently exists today the same three-tiered inner, outer, and "Court of the Gentiles" idea that existed in the temple courts of the time of Christ. People still think the church is a more sacred space than the Barnes & Noble coffee shop. I'd get questions like, "But what happens if someone from the clubs comes in and sees pagan Pete playing his tuba to 'This Is the Air I Breathe' and yet the night before he saw Pete smoking a joint? Won't that send the wrong message?" My response is, "What is the message you want to convey?" If you want to convey that someone who is up on the church stage has to prove a certain level of spiritual stability, then fine. That is your choice. But if you want to convey that your community is a place where anybody, in any phase of spiritual curiosity, can be in an environment in which God can touch their hearts, then you may try something like opening up your music group to include some Sojourners. (Though, yes, we'd definitely want the worship *leader* to be a missional member.) By the way, most of the musicians that we let play did come to faith.

Remember, biblical accountability (the attempt to spur fellow believers on toward love and good deeds, as well as the avoidance of sin) is only for those who are in leadership or who have committed to be a part of the missional people. In other words, Christ followers. Obviously, there are restraints on who can "lead" your community in worship, teaching, and so on, but we see Jesus sending out the Twelve, two by two, into the city to do ministry, even before they had come to full faith in the entire gospel message.

When we started our church, our neighbor Lori asked if she could help. Lori wasn't a Christian, but she loved us. She was spiritually curious and was genuine in her desire to serve. We'd known Lori and her family for years, and they were like family to us. I knew Lori was creative, crafty, and artistic, and she was great with kids. So I said, "I'd love to have you help with our children's ministry." I asked her to be the one who would craft the Bible lesson for the kids.

She freaked a little and said, "I don't know much about the Bible, so are you sure I'm the right person?"

"Not a problem, the Bible stories are easy to learn. Let's just take one a week and you and I will go over it together, then you can figure out how to teach it to the kids."

During the week, Lori would come over and we'd talk about David and Goliath or the woman at the well; I'd make sure she got the main points, and then she'd head off to plan the lesson. She was an important member of our initial "core group" well before she came to faith in Christ.

Let's consider the disciples whom Jesus called and used in ministry. When you think of the disciples, are they Christians? I always saw them as the first totally committed Christians. When Jesus called them to follow him on the beach, I always thought that was their come-to-the-altar moment.

I now see this is just bad theology.

In reality, the guys that Jesus asked to follow him had no clue what he was asking of them. They had some idea what following a rabbi might entail, but as we read about their confusion, it was clear they had no idea how it would transform their lives. What we *do* know is that even when Jesus spoke again and again of the new Kingdom, they didn't get it. They thought he'd be the next Jewish Terminator coming to kick the Romans out and reestablish the Jewish nation.

When Jesus sent his disciples out to minister—whether it was casting out demons, going two by two into houses to give blessings, or feeding large groups—they still didn't have clear or full faith. None of them had prayed a prayer, gone through church membership class, or even been to a church service. In fact, on the night before Jesus was going to entrust them to be the first pastoral leadership committee (after three years of being with Jesus), they still weren't even Trinitarian, and one was actually of the devil. In John 14:6–8, Jesus said, "No one comes to the Father except through me. If you really knew me, you would know my Father as well . . . ," and Phillip quickly said, "Lord, show us the father and that will be enough for us."

Today, if we met someone who loved Jesus but didn't know he was God, I doubt we would call that person a Christian, let alone use them in ministry. Yet Jesus did. I submit that for the entire time the disciples were with Jesus, they were what we would now call "Sojourners": spiritually disoriented God seekers.

Jesus had invited them into a school of apprenticeship and pushed them into spiritual activity as spiritual leaders, all before their faith was complete or fully formed. For Jesus, the process of discipleship was just that: *a process*. He wasn't concerned about who was "in or out," their level of knowledge or prior experience, lack of sin, or love of people. What he did know was that if he could get these guys involved or helping others alongside of him, they'd learn about him and his Kingdom, and someday they'd get the whole picture.

To stretch the point even more, notice how Jesus let someone that he knew was "out," namely Judas, hang around at the same level of leadership as the rest of the disciples. We've got to be able to put on this pair of inclusive glasses if we're going to be at peace with this new missional structure.

"Okay," you may ask, "so how do we control these participating Sojourners and avoid trouble?" Well, you don't. And it's okay. Sometimes it's messy, like the day Terry, our keyboard player, went off the heroin wagon. I was busy worshiping with my eyes closed when my friend nudged me and pointed to the stage. Terry had walked away from the keyboard and was making little animal symbols with his fingers on the overhead projector. I realized that Terry, who had been clean for two years, was now higher than the proverbial kite. I had to pull him off the stage in the middle of worship and take him out of our gathering time. Everyone in our community knew what was happening, and no one was shocked or repulsed. We were all just sad for Terry. You see, our entire congregation knew that in the pews and on the stage there were people, all at difficult stages, who were struggling to figure out Jesus. Our faith was in *God* to do the converting, and therefore we had no need to control our volunteers and the gathering. We all simply prayed for Terry, his recovery from addiction, and for his faith. Even messes are part of the Kingdom and may, in fact, be the best tools to reorient your people back to mission and to remind us why we do this church thing to begin with.

Coming to Faith

What is our hope for this missional model? It's simply that people might continue to move deeper into the life of the Kingdom. Notice how the color changes in Figure 12.2 as folks move from Sojourner to missional people. This signifies the conversion process. Because Sojourners have been around missional people and are drawn toward their values and their way of life, they're now starting to become like them, living out their values and beginning to love their God. It's a gradual merging rather than a pinpoint "Hurry and sign up today" conversion. We've found that when people come to faith like this, gradually and at their own pace, their faith is deeper and lasting.

The purpose of structure is to provide a reproducible, simple, and accessible framework through which the gospel can be experienced by both saint and Sojourner. This framework not only propels people closer together and deeper into the culture, but it also prevents the convictions from being watered down by nonparticipants.

The missional structure supports the incarnational approach we discussed in Chapter Eight. It makes the Discovery Zone available; inclusive community exists as saint and Sojourner are now united in the same community. Deep meaning can be modeled and experienced as Sojourners get to participate in the lifestyle and behaviors of the saints. People are influenced not by a position but simply by being impressed by the people they're with. And this structure provides a place for anyone to move toward faith at her own pace. In other words, this structure of incarnational community and missional congregation can deliver a much fuller picture of the gospel.

A quick but important point: If you recognize that you are a part of a traditional-attractional church structure, don't punt! The best response is to create the missional pyramid from scratch with a few missional people of your choice and start right where you are. If you leave, nothing beneficial will happen in your church. But if you—with a humble desire to influence or model a new way—launch out with a few friends while staying connected to your church, you'll not only enjoy the freedom of being on mission, you'll be able to influence and inspire more people within the existing structure to change.

When Matt and I work with attractional churches to help them become more missional, we never try to change or challenge the present structure. Instead, we ask for a small handful of would-be missionaries to pilot incarnational community. If it works, then we believe the grassroots success will spread to more people in the existing structure. Most pastors have no reason not to want this experiment to succeed. They want you to live out this calling, but part of their calling is to also hold the saints together. Structures don't change easily through challenge or critique. They change best as people within the organization change and model new approaches. So, instead of pointing your finger at your pastor or elder board, go live out this ancient way and pray for the larger community to eventually move forward with you. If you're a pastor and you're ready to move on this, we suggest the same thing. Call some friends together and begin a beautiful underground experiment. If it works, you'll have helped move your church into new territory. If it doesn't, you'll have a great time with a few friends. How bad can that be?

O

Reflection

o On Figure 12.3, locate yourself, your friends, family, neighbors, and the people you're connected to. Prayerfully get a sense of what God has been doing in these relationships.

O

13

THE HELLO EXPERIMENT

IN 1999, AN EXCELLENT MOVIE called *Patch Adams* came out. Robin Williams played the real-life character, Hunter "Patch" Adams. Adams had been inspired to become a doctor while being institutionalized for depression as a teenager. After some recovery time, Patch attended the Medical College of Virginia in the early 1970s and after graduation formed the Gesundheit Institute, which was dedicated to a more integrated, personalized approach to medicine. Having initially resisted public attention, he began receiving a flurry of media coverage about his unorthodox clinic in the mid-1980s, and he eventually wrote a book about his work in 1993.

Although the movie is dated, it's a great backdrop for helping us bring together all the concepts of the incarnational way we've been discussing in Chapters Eight through Twelve. In Patch Adams, we see the missionary life in two related processes. The first we call "living out," and the second we call "inviting in." Living out is about what *missional people* do. Inviting in is about how Sojourners move into our communities. These are the two overarching processes that bring missional people and Sojourners together. We discuss the practices of "living out" here and in Chapters Fourteen through Seventeen. We cover "inviting in" in Chapters Eighteen through Twenty-One.

Living Out

If you're a diagram person, go back and find the "Missional People" oval in Figure 12.1. *Living out* is focused on what missional people do together.

Living out is the natural and intentional process of making habits of four practices: leaving, living among, listening to, and loving with no strings attached. These four habits, if lived out by a given community of missional people, will help you have the right posture and be in correct position to gain the hearts of God-seeking Sojourners around you. You'll actually begin to change the normal programmed response of people toward the gospel, toward Christians, and maybe even toward the church. I'll let Patch explain.

Early in the movie, Patch is sitting with Truman, an intrigued but timid fellow med student. Truman is lamenting how people get stuck in ruts and says, "We start out so open and spontaneous, we're real individuals, and then somewhere along the way, we're drawn to conform as if we're conditioned by programmed response." Patch says, "Ah, but sometimes you can alter the programmed response, just by changing some of the conditions, altering the parameters. . . . Let me show you." Patch then leads Truman outside to start the experiment, announcing, "The goal of this experiment will be to break through programmed response by changing normal parameters and getting a new emotional response."

Patch begins the experiment by hanging upside down on a light pole and surprising an old lady who is walking down the sidewalk. As soon as their eyes meet, Patch nonchalantly says, "Hello." His upside-down approach catches her off guard, and she smiles and giggles to herself. "Victory!" Patch says. Truman is not impressed. As they continue to walk down the sidewalk, Patch goes on to tell him how he made twelve random phone calls and talked to one guy for three hours. As Patch explains the pleasure and power of just listening to people, he said, "If you want to help people, we have to dive into people, wade into the sea of humanity." He then takes Truman into a meat packers' convention and shows Truman how even vegetarians can make friends with meat packers simply by acting interested in meat. Next, Patch goes into the hospital and becomes a clown to a ward full of children who are suffering with cancer.

I've seen the movie many times, but I still can't keep the tears back as I watch Robin Williams blessing the lives of the children in the cancer ward (played by real kids with cancer). In each new spot, Patch changes the *programmed response* by simply being with people in their own worlds, by listening, and by creatively loving them. In the end, every person that Patch touches becomes a friend and loves to have him around.

Our churches could benefit from a similar experiment. People in America are not ignorant of Christianity. They've heard the message, seen our churches on every corner, they flick by our Christian TV shows, they see our fish symbols on the backs of our cars. They've seen so much of pop Christian culture that they have a programmed response to us: *Ignore, ignore, ignore.* What's needed is a change of parameters—something that will alter their emotional response.

In our first church plant in Portland, I formed a two-year connection with a UPS driver named Thad. Thad embodied his superhero name. He was an ultimate fighter, raw to the core, but always took time to turn off his truck and talk with me as he made his delivery run through our neighborhood. We had hundreds of conversations about God and life. One day, Thad invited me to his home to watch the Mike Tyson/Evander Holyfield fight. He said a few of his friends would be there and asked if I wanted to bring a few guys from the church. I, of course, said, "Yes." When we drove up to his house, we had to park a few hundred yards away because Thad had so many friends. When we walked in, Thad came over and announced to about eighty people, "Hey, everyone shut up. This is the Rev, my spiritual advisor!" Everyone made jokes about Thad having a spiritual anything, but most of them throughout the night initiated some conversation with us. Thad had communicated to his friends that "we belonged" with him, and therefore, we now belonged with his friends.

In order for us to change the incorrect assumptions that people have about God and his followers (their programmed responses), we've got to get to the point where they consider us one of them (the parameter change). To do this is not a matter of "evangelism" or "outreach" or "missions." It's a matter of *living out* like Jesus did.

Have you ever stopped to ponder how Jesus lived his first thirty years without drawing any attention to his divine nature? I don't know about you, but if I knew I was going to change the course of history, I'm sure it would have slipped out on occasion. I doubt I could have just lived a normal life. But Jesus did. He lived among people for three decades, developing the relational respect and trust of people in his community. Jesus "lived out." He left heaven, lived among us; he listened and loved unconditionally with no strings attached. He was nothing like what people thought he was. He altered the religious and secular response of every person he touched or talked to. He broke through programmed response because he changed the parameters, and in the end he did get a new emotional response. So can we!

Let's now look at each of the four habits separately, as we make our way through Chapters Fourteen to Seventeen.

14

LEAVING

WHEN WE COME TO this part of our church training seminar, often we ask all the pastors to grab their notebooks, coffee, muffins (all pastors eat muffins), and whatever else they have, and move outside. It's humorous to watch leaders, annoyed at having to leave their comfortable spots behind a table to go stand outside and listen to our training. That's a mini-version of the fight related to *leaving*, which entails intentionally giving up what is comfy, easy, and familiar and going somewhere else, doing something different, and giving up time so that we can connect with people.

Since the word *missional* theologically means "to be sent," *leaving* is where living like a missionary really begins. Leaving isn't just about going overseas. It's about *replacing personal or Christian activities with time spent building relationships with people in the surrounding culture.*

During our first year as a new church in Denver, we sent an e-mail out to our faith community telling them that we would be unable to meet in our usual spot for our weekly gathering. (We had been meeting in an old art gallery inside a mall.) We told them to meet out in front of our normal place at the same time as usual, and we would go as a group to another location in the mall. As people approached the door to our normal meeting area, we noticed discomfort and disappointment on their faces. One girl had brought her mother from out of town, and she appeared quite bothered when she saw the sign ("Go to the food court") on the door. She came up to me and said, "So we don't get to sing today?" I said, "No, not today, dear," and apologized to her mother.

So we had our ragtag gathering in the middle of the food court while all the "normal" mall people scurried around us. We moved about fifty chairs and pulled some tables together and then talked about our feelings of dis-comfort and disappointment, and how the ancient church had to deal with this uncomfortable feeling on a regular basis. They had to do church in the middle of the world. The point was obvious. The missional and incar-national church must be in the world all the time. The questions began to fly. "But shouldn't we be able to have our time, you know, as Christians?"

As you remember the incarnational structure and approach, you're probably intuiting that we're going to say "*No*," to this question.

When you think about some of the most intimate activities believers can do together, you might list prayer, worship, leadership development, fellowship, or communion. All these are things "believers" do. Yet, when you look at the biblical story, we find believers doing these Christian activities in the midst of Sojourners or "outsiders" all the time.

In 1 Corinthians 11:17–34, Paul angrily addressed the "Christian Church Gathering" for its communion practices. He essentially said, "You are messing up communion. Some of you are eating all the bread, some of you are getting drunk on the wine, while all the time there are poor peasants who are hungry and have no food to eat at all—watching." Paul warns them not to take the Lord's Supper in this manner.

I always thought that taking communion in an "unworthy" way meant that we should not participate if we had sinned. So I'd sit there for a while and beg for mercy and apologize and then wait a bit longer so people thought I was really contrite before I took the bread and wine. But the biblical mean-ing is clear. The hesitancy to take communion isn't about sin or analyzing how well we did during the week. If that's the case, then communion is based on works, which of course would fly in the face of the symbolic ele-ments of grace. The "unworthy" manner referred to doing religious things without concern for the common people who are observing. That's right; the most intimate Christian act of communion was often done in a more public setting than we imagine. About 99 percent of the miracles that Jesus and his disciples performed were done outside of a church building.

In the past, I once enjoyed a season in a charismatic denomination. My spiritual formation was greatly enhanced by the denomination's belief in the supernatural and their determination to "get their miracle." If you've grown up in that environment, you'll remember that at the end of every service you had an altar time. That's when you let the Holy Spirit have his way over the people who went forward for prayer, healing, and so on.

Once, during a leadership conference, the speaker asked every minister to come forward, and he told us that God was going to slay us in the Spirit. I'd been open to this in the past, but for whatever reason, God seemed to always pass over me. As the speaker had warned, everyone fell over, except me. I was like the ten-pin that just wouldn't go down. The minister looked perplexed and came over to me and gave it one more shot, but I just stood there, now smiling. He didn't think it was funny and applied a bit of "unnatural" pressure to my forehead and then gave me a pretty good nudge. Still no response, except I was starting to get a little ticked off. Then he whispered in my ear.

"Son, your lack of faith is keeping you from God's blessing."

I whispered back, "Maybe God's got bigger fish to fry than blessing a bunch of people who have been blessed their whole lives." I was out of there in a hurry and spent the evening at a local pub enjoying the company of the unblessed.

I'm not sure how we got where we are, but it's amazing that we think our most powerful times, our most intimate spiritual experiences, are supposed to happen within the comfortable confines of our church services. The biblical evidence is overwhelming and is crystal clear that God's power is most naturally meant to happen "out there"!

The early church did meet in secret; the church has done so in times of persecution throughout the world, and many still do to this day. Jesus also pulled his disciples away at times to give them a break and to debrief. That's okay, too. We're not saying that we shouldn't have private times with believers, but in early church times, the majority of the Christian activities were clearly done in plain view and for the benefit of the onlooking culture. They did meet privately, not out of separation theology, but because they had to. If God's church is to regain its influence in the world, we will have to get much more comfortable doing "our stuff" out there again.

So this is what leaving is all about. Simply stated, it's being "out there." I've learned that if I stay in my office to study, nothing happens. But whenever I intentionally or unintentionally plant myself at a local hangout, I run into people and conversations start, and at the end of the day I know that something Kingdom oriented has happened.

Here are a few examples of leaving, drawn from our life:

○ *Letting people live with you in your home for extended periods of time.* In the five years that we've lived in Denver, we've had people living with us more than four hundred of those days. Remember, I'm an introvert. Even though I get to stay in my home, for me having house guests is a form of leaving. I'm intentionally giving up my space, my time, my comfort for the sake of connecting with Sojourners.

○ *Having dinners or doing dinners out with Sojourners.* Not rocket science, but I'd almost always rather eat by myself or with just my family. Leaving is committing at least one night a week or one meal a week to Sojourners.

○ *Doing what you love with others.* Matt and I love to golf and mountain bike. We've made the habit of trying to do what we love to do with a Sojourner, if possible.

○ *Going out of your way to build relationships.* When I drive home after six meetings and eight cups of coffee, I look to see whose car is in the parking lot at our Starbucks. If it's a Sojourner I've been trying to include in my life, I'll pull over, go in, buy a quick coffee, try to make some good conversation, and then on my way out, throw my coffee away without even taking a sip.

○ *Looking for chances to talk.* When I have seen a neighbor outside on our street, I've specifically gone out to "get my mail" just so I could converse a bit more with him or her.

You get the point. Leaving is the first step in the missional and incarnational process.

○

Reflection

○ What are some things you love to do that would be easy to invite Sojourners to do with you?

○ What are some things that might be a struggle to give up in order to spend time connecting with people?

○

15

LISTENING

SEVERAL YEARS AGO, when we lived in Eugene, Oregon, I was doing my usual Starbucks thing, and over the course of a few months I got to know an employee named Jess. Jess used to hassle me about what I ordered, and we struck up a fun, over-the-counter rapport. She had the normal Eugene look: black hair, black eyes, black clothes, and enough studs and chains hanging from different points on her face that she could pose as a chandelier. Just to get to know her better, I would study there a lot, and often she would take her break and come over to talk to me about life, religion, or whatever. She was very open, but just like my fellow airplane passenger who blessed me, I could never find a crack in her armor. She loved life, had no interest in the church, had tons of friends, and generally enjoyed her daily routines.

One day I came in and tried to joke with her. Immediately, I could tell something was wrong. She didn't make eye contact, and it looked as though she might cry. I sat down, and after about an hour, I slipped her a little note across the counter asking if everything was all right. She wrote back and had a fellow employee deliver her reply. "No, I'm not doing too hot today. My father and brother just died this week. Suicide and a heart attack. . . . Sorry. I'm not my normal self." I knew that if I tried to console her, it would really make it hard for her at work. So I just left and went across the street to a florist shop. I bought two flowers and wrote her a note that said, "Sorry," and signed it, "From the Rev."

Several days went by, and I went back in for another cup of coffee. Before I got completely out of my car, I was literally mauled by Jess. She just hugged me and cried. As we took a half-hour break, she said, "Thanks for listening."

The second essential incarnational habit we hope to cultivate is simply *listening*. Listening is watching and sensitively responding to the unspoken and spoken needs of Sojourners in ways that demonstrate sincere interest.

When you hear the word *listen*, you probably think it's about setting up a coffee time and trying to ask probing questions. It may include that, but our kind of listening is really more about what you do with your eyes instead of just your ears.

I have a neighbor named Lenny who's not suburban by any means. He's covered with tattoos, he's a custom bike builder, and he runs a tattoo parlor out of his house. We instantly connected, and every time we talked, he mentioned that he didn't do drugs or alcohol. But after hearing the same "I don't do" speech, I started to listen between the lines. My curiosity told me that he must be doing other things he's not proud of, or this wouldn't be such a big deal.

As I watched his life, I learned that Lenny had a lot of free time and was pretty hungry for some good conversation. I noticed every time I opened my garage and started up my Harley, he would be over within a few minutes. Based on what I was "hearing" by watching his life, I surmised that Lenny would probably love to have a life coach, so I offered to trade him two tattoos and help customizing my old Harley for my time doing a full life assessment and personal gifts inventory for him. Not surprisingly, he jumped at the idea.

This issue of listening may sound easy, but it's quite a lost art. In the church planting world, we often start new churches by running a demographic of an area. The demographic can give many details about the area, like the average income, ethnic makeup, average age, size of schools, crime rates, or how much growth is expected. They gather the "data" and then pick a church planter to fit the "needs of the community." That's often the extent of their listening. The underlying belief is that a demographic match between the planter and the area is all we need to effectively target a ministry area.

This superficial type of listening is about generalities and stereotypes, and therefore it often misses the mark. Sure it can be helpful, but you can learn a lot more by sitting down in the local coffee shop for an hour.

Our church plant training is called Zer0, primarily because we're trying to instill a missionary posture in our leaders. The basis of missionary activity is to make *no* assumptions, zippo, *nada*, zero! Second Corinthians 5:16 says, "So from now on we regard no one from a worldly point of view." The context of this scripture reflects how we often view people based on superficial qualities. So listening in our context is about "knowing" the person.

Jesus, again, is our master and modeler. Notice how he dealt differently with every person he came into contact with. Whether it was the woman at the well, Nicodemus, Levi, Mary Magdalene, or the disciples, he listened and knew how to respond in a way that would affect their hearts. There were no pat answers, no formulas, no one-time offers. He listened and taught us that the smallest element of any culture is an individual person. Each person is unique. Their experiences, traumatic moments, family background, ethnic heritage, and church experience all make up how they interpret relationship and processes faith and belief. Whenever we skip over the listening piece, we've failed.

o

_____

Reflection

o We recommend that you take one person out for coffee and work on "only" asking questions. Note what happens when you focus all your attention on someone for an hour.

_____

o

16

LIVING AMONG

WHILE MY PARENTS WERE growing up, they were part of a holiness tradition that had a heightened focus on "not sinning" and, in fact, not getting within 10 miles of the smell of sin. No dice on movies, no dice at all for that matter. No art, bowling, alcohol, tobacco use of any kind, no dancing, no playing cards, no drums in church, no saying "Darn" because that's a derivative of *dang*, and *dang* is a Latin ancestor or third cousin to *damn*. Same with *shoot, shucks, crap, geez*, and *cripes*. I'm not sure where they found some loopholes, but my uncle could say, "Dad gum," and all my parents and relatives played the card game Rook. I think they told me once that the Raven on the top of the Rook box is a Greek expression of the dove or Holy Spirit bird. I bought it at the time, but not any more. After all these years, I finally found out that Rook was okay because it has no face cards. You know, no king other than God, no queen, as she's a seductress, and that poor suicidal Jack was too emotionally unstable to look at.

This may be a humorous story that you can identify with, but if you decide to really be incarnational, you will have to deal with some very serious tensions. Most of them center around the question, "What is holiness?" This issue causes families to break up, churches to split, great young church planters to be mistrusted, and it is the primary reason that people outside the church think our God is like an old, senile, out-of-touch beat cop!

For whatever reason, the church at large has theologized the idea of personal holiness to exclude normal interaction with the world. Many churches we work with have an alarming theology of "extraction" that creates a Christian peer pressure to move away from the world in all its forms. To these people, the world is dirty, dark, intimidating, and evil.

This issue of "How incarnational should an incarnational community be?" is why we must align our theology around the call of mission. This third habit of incarnational people: the habit of *living among*, means *participating in the natural activities of the culture around you, with whimsical holiness.*

One particular church wanted us to help them become more evangelistic. While with them, we realized that about 50 percent of their families homeschooled their children. Now, don't get me wrong, there are a few places where I would opt to homeschool my kids, but this church wasn't in any of them. They were located in a small mountain town in central Colorado known for its cherries and peaches and other happy, normal things. We tried to somehow move them toward mission, but it's mission impossible if people are unwilling to integrate their families into the fabric of society.

As you can tell, this issue of holiness or perceived holiness is the theological elephant in the room. If the church is to move out of irrelevance, this one issue must be settled both theologically and practically. Let's try to simplify the issues. The question of whether we "should" be in the world is pretty easy to reconcile. Christ addressed the issue this way. He told us in Matthew 5:13 that we were to be "salt and light." We've heard enough sermons on this to know that salt is a preserving agent, and it also releases flavor. The metaphor screams for our intimate proximity to those in need of preserving any taste of something great. In 1 John 2:6, we're confronted with the bottom line: "This is how we know we are in him: Whoever claims to live in him must walk as Jesus did." Obviously, to walk as Jesus did means we not only have freedom to but were commanded to live in the world like Christ did.

The next question becomes, "What activities of culture can we participate in?"

First Corinthians 10:23–31 helps us. "Eat anything sold in the meat market without raising questions of conscience, for 'the earth is the Lord's, and everything in it.' If some unbeliever invites you to a meal and you want to go, eat whatever is put before you without raising questions of conscience." Earlier in the same book, we find Paul's personal defense: "To the Jew I became like a Jew, to win the Jews. To those under the law I became like one under the law (though I myself am not under the law), so as to win those under the law. To those not having the law, I became like one not having the law (though I am not free from God's law, but am under Christ's law), so as to win those not having the law. To the weak I became weak, to win the weak. I have become all things to all men so that by all possible means I might save some. I do this for the sake of the gospel, that I may share in its blessings" (1 Corinthians 9:20–23).

The point is clear. To become like those without the law meant that Paul could overlook rules and regulations that would have otherwise governed his life under Jewish law. If they weren't an issue to the pagans, Paul could participate freely as long as he didn't transgress clear sin issues or his own personal conscience.

Last week, I attended an engagement celebration for one of our village leaders. He had just asked a Denver Bronco cheerleader to be his bride. The party was downtown in a nice hotel and was full of their friends—cheerleaders, professional lacrosse players, and many of his village community. At age forty, I feel privileged any time I get asked to hang with the "youngsters," and it was pretty fun to watch our young men navigate the tension of beautiful women, wine, and more beautiful women.

During the evening, I gave a toast and offered my best bottle of wine to the engaged couple. I read a card that my wife and I had written and spoke of the couple's faith and how important they had become to us and the Adullam community. It was a great moment to be able to enjoy this celebration with a mix of our community and all their non-Adullam people. There was great synergy, and our young community of Christ followers were the last ones to leave the place. We all commented on how we "outpartied" the partiers. As we walked out together, we had a great sense of love for each other, and deep down, we all knew that being in the world, together, was a great privilege. After the evening was over, the newly engaged bride-to-be mentioned how surprised some her friends were to find out that I was her pastor. One of the couples even asked if I would be willing do their premarital counseling.

Sharing our friends, sharing fun, sharing food, and an opportunity to minister to a young couple. Not a bad night. I think even though most of us see the beauty of this type of freedom, we still find it hard to give permission to ourselves and others to feast, dance, and enjoy people.

Incarnational life requires that we contextualize all the "warnings" found in the epistles with the larger context of the life of Jesus as recorded in the Gospels. In other words, we're going to have to learn all the things we *can* do instead of limiting ourselves based on a few things we're warned to avoid.

Let me give you yet another angle. Jesus and Paul both mention things that we're not to do. If we do those things (gluttony, drunkenness, fornication, and so on), then we know that we are sinning, correct? I think we'd all agree, *Yes*. But Jesus and Paul also told us we should *do* certain things, and when we don't do them, would we call that sin as well? We are told to take care of the poor and the least of these, to love our enemies and pray for them. We're told to love our wives as Christ loved the church; to be subject to one another; to give generously to everyone as they have need, to . . . Should I keep going, or have we had enough? The list is far longer on the things we're told to do than the things we're told to avoid.

Based on the things Jesus asked us to do and to avoid, I believe that we'd be well served to offer a new perspective on holiness, one that takes into account both sides of the equation. Try this out: What if *whimsical holiness* is simply "being like Jesus . . . with those Jesus would have been with"? How might this definition of holiness change the way we view people and live our lives?

You might be wondering if the people we're living among occasionally go too far, or if things get out of control when we're among a celebration of life around good food and wine? Of course! That's why we included in our definition of "living among" the word *whimsy*.

Whimsy is the ability to laugh, make light of, or downplay the words, behaviors, and worldview of Sojourners that might offend. Whimsy is deeply tied to our discussion of *posture* as we remember that behavior doesn't change until the heart changes. Whimsy, therefore, allows you to be with people regardless of their angle of life without casting any judgment their way. It paves the way for them to feel comfortable enough to be themselves, feel loved, and dignified as human beings. It's not making an issue out of anything that's not the main issue. That simply means we don't flinch at sin or bad language or nasty T-shirts or crude music or a Sojourner who overindulged. Whimsy may be the missing element of Christlike love in today's world. It's the essence of missional posture that helps gain someone's heart so that, someday, their behavior may also change.

Remember, Jesus came not to judge the world but to save the world. You can't save the ones you judge. You can only save the ones you're connected to. Loving the person doesn't mean you're condoning their behavior. It just means you'll be a trusted friend. At one time, our next-door neighbors were slowly coming toward our community. I biked with the husband, and our wives did a lot of fun things together. One day the wife met me at our mailbox, and as she struck a funny girly pose, she said, "What do you think?"

"About what?" I answered.

"My new boobs."

Remember when I said that all the changes in our world are causing us a lot of tension—well, this is what I meant. Not wanting to be rude, I said, "Well, they appear to be just fine. Are you happy with them?" I felt like I was talking about her new vacuum cleaner. After our conversation, my twelve-year-old daughter, who happened to be there during the whole escapade, asked me what I thought about people getting fake boobs. I can't remember what I said, but I'm sure it was stupid.

A day later, my neighbor called me and apologized for being so "up front" (forgive the pun) in front of my daughter. I laughed it off and told her it was no big deal. I said, "Actually, it's prompted us to consider doing a study on how to lead our kids morally in the world we now live in. Obviously, our kids are going to have to deal with a lot of issues we didn't have to." My neighbor responded, "We'd definitely come."

As I pondered why she would have been that honest with me and still be willing to be in a neighborhood discussion group, I sensed it had a lot to do with whimsy. I wasn't offended by her breast augmentation; I didn't belittle her or give her my opinion. I minimized or overlooked the surface issues so that at some point we could get to the real issues of her self-esteem.

The next week, we put out an invite that became our first official "village." The first night, I told the neighborhood group that even though I would facilitate the discussion, Cheryl and I weren't the experts. We said, "We struggle like anyone with this topic, so we're all in this together."

You can see that if holiness is defined as avoiding the world of the fake boobs, tattoos, card games, or a nice glass of merlot; if we're constantly concerned with what we *don't do* instead of what we *can do*, we'll miss out on truly being *followers* of Jesus!

The issue isn't so much about how far you can go to "do evangelism." Its more about whether or not we will enlarge our view of discipleship to include behaving like Jesus did with the types of people Jesus would always have made a priority. You can't be a follower of Jesus unless you actually follow him. Whimsy is the posture we take that allows people to be themselves. Holiness is that quiet inner posture that shines through and subversively witnesses of an alternative way to live. Whimsy implies that you can seamlessly interact in the culture with ease, humor, love, and holiness without being swayed away from *clear* biblical boundaries.

This freedom modeled by Jesus is what has allowed our worship leader to work part time as a poker dealer, investing in a community and building relationships in a subculture that very rarely sees any light of the gospel penetrate its ranks. It's Jesus' life that has given me permission to start a brewing club and teach men about the great monastic traditions and values. The model of Christ is how I model my leadership to others.

Matt and I work with many denominations that have a ministerial code of ethics that prohibit ministers from consuming alcohol. The issue usually relates to, "What behaviors are acceptable for leaders?" It's inferred that leaders should model a higher level of discipline as well as avoiding any appearance of impropriety that may bring reproach upon the larger group. Because of this one issue, many gifted pastors and leaders have had either to lie about what they do to build relationship with people in culture or leave the denomination.

The issue really is one of leadership and understanding that avoiding the world is not necessarily the highest form of Christlikeness. Leaders are faced with tough challenges and tensions that they must learn to navigate so that they can model the balance that Christ demonstrated. Rather than extracting people from the world, there is an opportunity for leaders to influence culture and model a new way forward. If the leadership of the church doesn't show the way, the church will continue to be an irrelevant subculture doomed for extinction.

Hear this great prayer of Jesus: "My prayer is not that you take them out of the world but that you protect them from the evil one" (John 17:15). May it be so in our day!

○

Reflection

○ What activities in the surrounding culture have we as Christians been afraid to participate in?

○ List some activities in our culture today that you think Jesus would avoid.

○ "My prayer is not that you take them out of the world but that you protect them from the evil one" (John 17:15). How might Jesus' prayer speak to the way you live?

○

17

LOVING WITHOUT STRINGS

WHAT WOULD YOU DO WITH $181 million? Why do I ask? Well, it's the amount of the Powerball jackpot this week. I've asked a few people this question, and every person, whether Christian or not, poor, middle class, or wealthy, all list a bunch of people they would love to help. Last week I woke up from a great dream in which I won the $181 million jackpot. I showed up at our church gathering and asked people to take 10 minutes and write down all their debt (houses, cars, credit cards, school loans, and anyone they were indebted to). The next scene of the dream was of Matt and me sitting on stools in front of our people, encouraging them to come take communion and then bring us their list of debts. We formed two lines and began writing checks to cover all their debt. Eventually the place erupted with tears of joy. Everyone was hugging each other; grown men were jumping around like boys; and one guy asked if he could go find people in the fitness center where we were meeting to see if we could pay off their debt too. I said, "What the heck. I've still got about $80 million!"

Then I woke up. I was bummed, to say the least.

I had just lived 10 minutes in a dream every one of us would love to be a part of in the real world. The closest real-life experience I can imagine is watching *Extreme Home Makeover* on my 42-inch plasma TV. I cry every time.

Did you know that we're all created with a built-in desire to love the world, to bless people? It's the main job description of a Christian. Way back when the term *emerging church* meant that the church was really emerging, God set up a deal with humanity.

Genesis 12:1–3: "The Lord had said to Abram, "Leave your country, your people and your father's household and go to the land I will show you. I will make you into a great nation and I will bless you; I will make your name great, and you will be a blessing. I will bless those who bless you, and whoever curses you I will curse; and all peoples on earth will be blessed through you."

An old *Webster's Dictionary* says that *to bless* means "to ask divine favor for a person" or "to make happy or prosperous or gladden." To be blessed means to "enjoy great happiness, blissful, receiving comfort or joy, anything that gives happiness or prevents misfortune." This isn't about the "name it, claim it," health-and-wealth theology that dupes people into thinking that God is bound by his divine laws to be the sugar daddy to his spoiled, self-serving, trust-fund children. Biblical blessing is the tangible favor of a personal God who loves humankind and desires to offer his life to them.

It's best understood in the Hebrew term *Shalom.* "Shalom," said as a greeting or benediction, references one person's desire to see the peace of God touch every aspect of another's life. It's a holistic blessing that calls for action by the one granting the blessing. This idea is explained in James 2:14–17: "What good is it, my brothers, if a man claims to have faith but has no deeds? Can such a faith save him? Suppose a brother or sister is without clothes and daily food. If one of you says to him, 'Go, I wish you well; keep warm and well fed,' but does nothing about his physical needs, what good is it?"

Blessing, therefore, is more than just a passive wish for someone's good. Blessing requires action. It's the essence of God's call to Abraham to help the world—his world. It's most often directed to a nation, family, or community, instead of for an individual. Blessing is given to God's community, for the global community.

Ultimately, God's offer to us to share his blessing with others is how we find our deepest sense of personal meaning and satisfaction. Jesus said it this way: "Whoever wants to save his life will lose it, but whoever loses his life for me and for the gospel will save it" (Mark 8:35). This wasn't a call to drudgery and painful sacrifice as much as it was Jesus' way of saying, "Sir, catch a clue. If you really want to have a blast, then free up some time and money and go bring a smile to someone's face. Relieve someone's pressure. Surprise someone with a gift." Jesus mentions blessing as giving sight to the blind, captives being set free, debts being paid off, food for the hungry, friends for the lonely, meaningful employment for the discouraged and self-doubting, rest for the weary, and anything else that could be felt or touched on terra firma. The Tangible Kingdom! Blessing wasn't just nice things you said to make people forget about their problems. It was actually doing something about their problems.

You might be thinking, "But Hugh, we only have limited time. I'm so busy that I barely have time to brush my teeth. If I only have a few moments to influence someone, shouldn't I cut to the chase and just tell them about God? I'd love to serve them, but the church is to be more than a social agency. Our ultimate goal is to get them to heaven . . . isn't it?" (I love to put words in your mouth.)

If you have any questions related to this, it may mean that you're still missing the point of blessing. That is, we think God tells us to serve in order to get people to respect us or like us so that they'll accept our God. The real essence of biblical blessing is that it's done with *no strings attached*. Hopes, desires, fervent prayer, yes—but no strings at all attached.

If, starting with the Old Testament, you made a list of all the times in scripture that people are blessed without any coercion, you'd find a few hundred direct references to blessings that are given without any connection to "getting saved." In the New Testament, we have Jesus feeding four thousand, then five thousand people, without giving an "invitation." He healed many people, raised at least one from the dead, picked up the wine tab for a few hundred, and then ultimately carried the sins of the whole world on his bloody back to a cross that was offered to everyone.

People aren't stupid; they know when they're receiving something with strings attached. Ever get an evening call telling you that you'd won a free vacation? I've had more than few, and there's *always* a catch.

A few years back, I was running a half-marathon through the redwoods, and someone held out a cold bottle of water to me. I recall being annoyed that the dude didn't think to take the top off for me. Let me tell you, after running 10 miles, taking a plastic cap off a bottle is about as easy as fixing a broken antenna on a lunar space module. My annoyance got worse when I realized that the guy had taped a gospel tract to the side of the bottle. Like I'm going to stop and have a devotional time, turn around, and come to Jesus right there. *Pu-lease.*

Learning to receive God's free, no-strings-attached offer and then graciously living a life to extend blessing to others without charge and without expectation is different. When we become comfortable with unconditional love, I think we will find that it does witness correctly to who God is. And it's a power that naturally draws people in.

In the book *The Shaping of Things to Come*, by Alan Hirsch and Michael Frost, the authors provide a metaphor of how the blessing of the gospel naturally attracts others. The authors are from Australia, and in the vast Outback region ranchers are unable to control their livestock using fences. It's just too big to keep the fences intact. The alternative approach is to simply provide accessible wells where the animals learn to find relief for their thirst. The ranchers know that if the well is the only place of refreshment and survival, the animals will naturally stay close.[1]

Blessing without coercion has this same unique power to draw. We may not always feel it when building a deck for someone, shoveling snow, helping out financially, watching a neighbor's kids, opening our home, or giving gifts, but these habits and activities do create a well that people will eventually gravitate toward. There's no way to shortcut it, minimize the sacrifice that may be required, or pawn off the duties on someone else. Just as people brought their sick and dying friends and family out in the streets for the disciples to pass by and bless, so will people in our vortex of Kingdom love. *Vortex* represents the web of relationships that are within tangible touch of our people. Just as there's no belief without belonging, there's no belonging without blessing. Remember, the goal of living out is to "belong with them." Living out habits are not steps to evangelism. They are habits of a Christ follower who wants to live faithfully like Jesus lived. The rest is up to him. We suggest that if you focus on these habits, you won't have to worry about the rest. People will begin to love you, respect you, and take your life and the life of your community seriously. You will also find that your spiritual life finally makes sense, because each habit breaks down your human selfishness. Each of the four habits of living out has a corresponding internal resistance. It's a good place to center your prayers.

> Selfishness is the enemy of "Leaving."
>
> Fear is the enemy of "Living Among."
>
> Arrogance is the enemy of "Listening."
>
> Expectations are the enemy of "Loving."

Let developing these habits be your prayer and your commitment to God. These words from Henri Nouwen sum it up nicely:

> More and more, the desire grows in me simply to walk around, greet people, enter their homes, sit on their doorsteps, play ball, throw water and be known as someone who wants to live with them. It is a

privilege to have the time to practice this simple ministry of presence. Still, it is not as simple as it seems.

My own desire to be useful, to do something significant, or to be part of some impressive project is so strong that soon my time is taken up by meetings, conferences, study groups and workshops that prevent me from walking the streets. It is difficult not to have plans, not to organize people around an urgent cause and not to feel that you are working directly for social progress.

But I wonder more and more if the first thing shouldn't be to know people by name, to eat and drink with them, to listen to their stories and tell your own and to let them know with words, handshakes and hugs that you do not simply like them—but truly love them.[2]

○

Reflection

○ Describe how selfishness, fear, arrogance, and expectations can hinder true blessing.

○ Pretend for a moment that your church has 50 percent of its budget to give directly to needs in your community. What would you do?

○

18

INVITING IN

AS WE TURN THE CORNER into "inviting in," let me remind you of where we've been. In Chapters Fourteen through Seventeen we focused on what *missional people* do to *live out* the gospel together. Leaving, listening, living among, and loving without strings are the practices that help us draw the hearts of the sojourning world.

We turn the corner with this question: What happens when it works? When we see people moving toward us? When people start inquiring about our lives? What are we "inviting them into"?

To answer these questions and a few others, we look now at the three spheres of incarnational life that we hope to invite people into. These spheres form the essence of the Tangible Kingdom.

The Spheres of Incarnational Community

During a recent international consultation on "community" that brought together monastic orders, house churches, submonastic orders who work among the poor, and "normal" joes like us who get to thrash out church in the Western suburbs, the entire group realized that everyone shared, in some form or fashion, three primary aspects of incarnational life. As illustrated in Figure 18.1, they are communion, community, and mission.

Figure 18.1   The Primary Spheres of Incarnational Community.

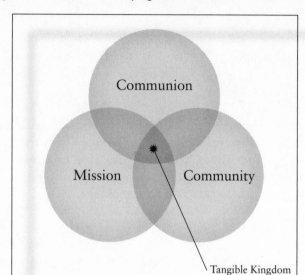

Communion represents "oneness"—those things that make up our communal connection and worship of God. *Community* represents aspects of "togetherness"—those things we share as we form our lives together. And *mission* represents "otherness"—the aspects of our life together that focus on people outside our community.

We believe that whenever you see a group of people who find a rhythm or balance among communion, community, and mission, you will always find the Kingdom. It will be tangible!

Community is everything related to how God works his redemptive ways among people. Ephesians 2:12 gives us a glimpse into the depth of the early faith communities. Paul is speaking to people who "were separate from Christ, excluded from citizenship in Israel and foreigners to the covenants of the promise, without hope and without God in the world." These were clearly people who had not felt a part of the Jewish spiritual heritage and who therefore felt a deep divide socially with these "God-people." In Acts 2, we get a more detailed picture of how different people were who were coming to faith and trying to navigate their way into a new community; Acts 2:9 lists "Parthians, Medes and Elamites; residents of Mesopotamia, Judea and Cappadocia, Pontus and

Asia, Phrygia and Pamphylia, Egypt and the parts of Libya near Cyrene; visitors from Rome (both Jews and converts to Judaism); Cretans and Arabs." After Peter gives a lengthy sermon, we read in 2:41, "Those who accepted his message were baptized, and about three thousand were added to their number that day."

When talking about community and otherness, I think we sometimes forget that all the passages on community, "one-anothers" that we're called to weren't written to just white evangelicals, or Hispanic communities, or affinity-based small groups. The context is actually quite in opposition to what we're used to. They speak to people who were divided by ethnic lines, deep traditions, skin color, and alternative worldviews. The call of community isn't about finding people just like us, or at the exclusion of any people. Community in the biblical sense is clearly about unlike people finding Christ at the center of their *inclusive* life together. Thus, issues of community reflect powerful dynamics of how God brings very diverse people together for his glory and his witness in the world.

The second sphere, communion, represents those things related to our intimate connection with God through spiritual formation, worship, and prayer. These issues relate to becoming "one" with Christ, thus the word *Oneness*. Traditionally, many of these aspects are linked to a corporate gathering at which people come together to experience oneness with God, but as we discuss, it does not have to be bound by a weekly church service.

The third sphere, mission, represents God's invitation to every Christ follower to participate in his work to bring redemption to the whole world. We call this "otherness" because this aspect of the Kingdom represents everything that's not directly about us and that makes God's way *tangible* to real people and real issues in the world.

In Adullam, we put much emphasis on helping people create and participate in incarnational communities. It's not just an attempt to start a bunch of small groups all over the city. We believe that unless people experience all three elements together and fight for this Tangible Kingdom, they won't grow as disciples of Christ, and Sojourners won't be moving toward God.

Most of us look at the three spheres of Kingdom life without much argument. We've talked about aspects of these a hundred different ways, in thousands of sermons, and have created an extensive list of programs to attempt to move people toward them. So why does it seem so hard to integrate these spheres into our lives and our churches?

The answer is, quite simply, that there are real barriers to connecting these three spheres with our own lives. Galatians 5:17 says it this way: "For the sinful nature desires what is contrary to the Spirit, and the Spirit what is contrary to the sinful nature. They are in conflict with each other, so that you do not do what you want." So if you really want to know why people just go to church without engaging community or mission, you don't need to look far. It's not that the pace of the world is too fast or the forces of darkness are too hard to fight against. It's that we are fighting against ourselves.

Barriers to Incarnational Community

Let's take a closer look at the barriers that keep us stuck in our one-dimensional Christianity.

Individualism

The barrier to moving from communion to community usually centers on individualism (illustrated in Figure 18.2).

Individualism is a deep-seated WestMod bias that fights against commitment to anything that doesn't directly serve our individual interests. Most specifically, this relates to our interaction with people. Although we may want a deeper sense of community, we're not going to make the

Figure 18.2   The Barrier of Individualism.

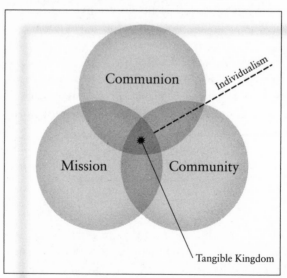

changes in our lives so that we can commit to it. People come to Adullam all the time because they hear about our villages and our emphasis on incarnational community and then struggle like geese flying through a hailstorm to see the intangible become tangible. As we help people process their struggle, we see some consistent patterns. We hear of time management issues, overcommitment to extended family, prioritizing a favorite weeknight TV show, or the constraints of children. Some symptoms of individualism are quite easy to get over, and some are very legitimate and need patient coaching. This is a systemic issue that keeps our Western-oriented churches from experiencing the joys of Eastern community. Changes to our modern propensity toward individualism won't come through preaching or programs. Deeply engrained habits only change as they are replaced with new habits. We win out over individualism by discipling togetherness, through gentle confrontation, and by eliminating spiritual services that allow people to remain autonomous or invisible.

In Adullam, we never reference our relationship with God as "personal." We speak of it as "communal." As people find our Gathering, I often see them go find a seat to wait for the service to begin, while our normal community is eating, drinking, and relating to each other. Even though I feel pain to go and talk to them, I force myself to remain where the community is happening. My hope is that the awkwardness of sitting by yourself waiting for the "service" to begin will eventually be overshadowed by the pain of missing out on new relationships.

For people to find inclusive community, they need to be allowed to hunger for it. Mother Teresa said this: "If we have no peace, it is because we have forgotten that we belong to each other."[1]

Consumerism

The barrier to moving from communion to mission centers on consumerism. (See Figure 18.3.)

Whereas individualism keeps us from biblical community, *consumerism* keeps us from being able to participate in God's mission to the world. Consumerism is based on the belief that I can't help others until I help myself, that my own wants and needs trump the needs of others. During an Adullam village a few months ago, one new mom was joking about how much more they provided for their first child than their second. The first got every toy imaginable, special food, and brand new clothes. The second one got a pot and kettle, and few wooden spoons for toys, and hand-me-down clothes. We all laughed, because we'd learned the same thing. That is, our perceived needs are not always the same as

Figure 18.3   The Barrier of Consumerism.

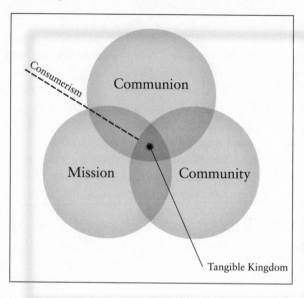

our actual needs. Filling perceived needs costs a lot more than filling actual needs, and if perceived needs don't get adjusted, they can render you in debt and unable to get what you really need. This is why some debt is called "consumer debt." It's debt you incur completely unnecessarily because you've provided for yourself items and luxuries you don't really need.

Church can be a huge consumer trap. We provide large, comfortable worship centers, encourage pastoral staff to give us everything we need spiritually, and, at the end of the day, we don't have any money or time left to extend blessing and resources toward *mission*.

Just as discipling togetherness requires that we limit individualistic options for people's spiritual growth, we must in like fashion limit how much comfort and convenience we provide people if we want to see them have time, money, and energy for mission. Several weeks ago I was with a couple that has struggled to find their place in Adullam. I asked the husband what he'd really love to do and he said, "I'd love to be a part of a choir where I can join my love of music with people in the church." This man was not "old school"; in fact, he's quite progressive and agrees with how outward oriented Adullam is, but he was still hoping to find a meaningful program connection with people. As much as I'd love to see him find it inside Adullam, and even provide it, I had to push back and call him to connect his passion for music out in a civic choir or secular context.

Personally, I'm getting to the point where I'm tired of my office always being a Starbucks! I want a quiet building all my own, with my own coffee maker, a cool place to have leaders pray and study together, and that Matt and I can call our home. But every time we consider this, we think of the money it would cost, and we realize that we can always spend that money on real needs and real people. We all fight the same consumer tendencies, and we must struggle as a community to limit what we need inside the church so others can get what they need in the world.

Materialism

The barrier to moving from community to mission is materialism. (See Figure 18.4.)

Both consumerism and individualism hit pretty close to home for most people living in Western industrial societies and bleed deeply into how

Figure 18.4   The Barrier of Materialism.

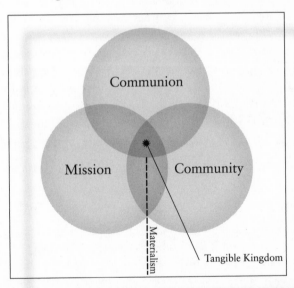

we do church. Materialism is not all that dissimilar to consumerism, but it is more closely related to the struggle of Sojourners to tangibly be a blessing in the world. For example, often, when Sojourners enter into our Tangible Kingdom vortex through community, they've found friends and are moving toward faith, but they still haven't adjusted their lives toward God's blessing in the world. Because they have had little focus on God or personal stewardship, they are weighed down in debt and the extra work that is required to keep up. Whereas consumerism holds some aspect of entitlement ("This church should provide . . . ; this leader should provide . . ."), materialism is simply about wanting stuff.

Even though Sojourners love to help people, they are often in the same boat because they've shipwrecked their personal finances and time schedules. Just as there are massive possibilities dormant within the consumer church, there are even more opportunities to bless the world if we can help materialistic Sojourners quickly reorient their lives around helping people.

I have a friend in Las Vegas who is a casino developer. He's made some great strides with God over the years, and we've connected his resources into a mission to South America. It's interesting, according to the Barna Group, Christians on average give 2.9 percent to the church and church-related ministries. Sojourners and pagans give 2.8 percent to charities around the world.[2]

Yes, it does show that Christians are generally uninspired to give to the existing church, but it also shows that the heart of giving is resident in every person. Just as Christians need to be discipled past individualism and consumerism, Sojourners can be discipled into mission. The way to mature past these is fairly straightforward:

> The more we do "together," the less *individualistic* we'll be.
>
> The more we become "one" with Christ, the less *consumer oriented* we'll be.
>
> The more we do for "others," the less *materialistic* we'll be.

We hope you now have a good idea of the practices of *living out* and what we're *inviting* people *into*. That is, people who integrate inclusive community, communion, and mission. In Chapters Nineteen through Twenty-One we unpack more of the practices that we ask people to share in each of these three Kingdom spheres.

○

Reflection

○ As you look at the three redemptive spheres of incarnational community, which ones feel comfortable and which ones seem elusive to you? Why?

○ How do you struggle with the barriers between the spheres? Reflect specifically on consumerism and individualism.

○

19

TOGETHERNESS

WHAT WE DO IN THIS CHAPTER and in Chapters Twenty and Twenty-One is pull the three spheres identified in Chapter Eighteen apart and suggest habits or rhythms that may help disciple people into this intentional life. We begin here with the sphere of community. Figure 19.1 shows the rhythms of community: sharing *friends, food,* and *life.*

Sharing Friends

In 1999, sociologist Ray Oldenburg wrote an eye-opening book called *The Great Good Place.*[1] In it, he offers a compilation of essays about those places in America where everybody knows your name. What Oldenburg calls "the third place" is different from home and work (the first and second places, respectively). The "third place" is somewhere people can relax, in good company, on a regular basis. They are places of familiarity, where people can find and make friends. Starbucks has formed their international purpose statement around this idea. They want to become the "the third place" for everyone.

In the past, folks built front porches on their homes, streets were narrower, and people could connect just by sitting out in their front yard. Conversation happened, and people became friends. Today, everything is

Figure 19.1   The Rhythms of Community.

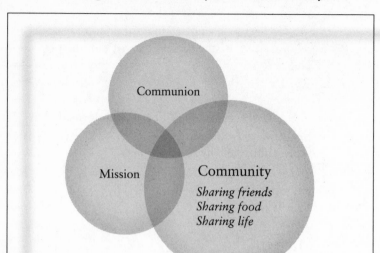

stacked against us. The worst mistake has been that Christians have tried to make their church programs or worship services their third place. The key is that third places need to be in public zones.

After I had trained a group of women's leaders at a large church, one of the leaders came up to me and was obviously a bit hot under the collar. "Okay," she said, "I'm a little miffed and I need to tell you that I just don't see how I can do all this. I help run the women's leadership here at the church, I lead several Bible studies, I disciple a few women during the week, I do aerobics here at the church several times a week, and now you want me to add sharing life, sharing food, and blah, blah, blah" (*her words exactly*). "How am I supposed to do all this?"

Realizing that other women were watching and listening to our chat, I said, "What would happen if instead of doing your aerobics here at the church, you just did them at a local 24-Hour Fitness with the same ladies?" She was silent for a moment, and then she said, "Well, I guess that might work, and it may even save me some time. I could lead our Bible study in the coffee shop that's connected to the front desk area of the club. And just in case we connect with some unchurched ladies, we could invite them to join us for both the workout and the study." Then she skipped away as if she had just discovered the key to the universe. It's really not that difficult, just different.

One of our couples met a thirtysomething at the poker table in a Colorado mountain casino. Like the *Cheers* bars of old, the poker table has become for many the new third place. "He seemed like a lost soul," the man said in describing his new friend to his wife. A month or two later, they met him again at the same poker table. (What are the odds of that happening?) Soon golf was planned, and a friendship formed. Not once did this couple invite him to Adullam. But they did invite him to dinner, home poker games...into their lives. He showed up at their village a couple times, but he wasn't ready to engage with a larger community. A couple of years later, when he *was* ready, he started showing up. Then his girlfriend came, then one of her friends. In the course of entering community, they're all heading in the right direction—at their own pace.

In Adullam, we find that good things just seem to happen when we share spontaneously. If you need a place to start, begin by taking up a hobby that naturally puts you in third places. Adjust your routine to include meeting friends, both saint and Sojourner, in public places that are comfortable for everyone. I think you'll find that community begins to take shape, naturally.

Sharing Food

What's the big deal with food? Again, go through the Gospels and now note how many stories include sharing food. I can tell you the percentage, but I'd be denying you a great opportunity to see something that is so often missed when we look at God's mission in the world.

The fact that there's almost always food around isn't surprising, since our scriptures are written in an entirely Eastern context. In Eastern cultures, food, the home, and hospitality are the center of culture, life, and relationships. Food, like music, is something anyone can share and enjoy with others, even if they can't speak the same language. Food is tangible and gives you something to do when you're socially nervous. Food relieves tension. It brings complete strangers to the same table without any instructions or barriers. Food satisfies our greatest physical need and allows people to show creativity and thoughtfulness. It invites participation and is welcome in any setting.

Furthermore, God uses the banquet table analogy to speak about heaven, salvation, and evangelism. Christ uses the phrase "bread of life" to refer to himself. God even brings back the tree of life found in Genesis and plants it right in the middle of heaven and causes it to produce a different fruit every month!

In Adullam, every eight weeks or so, we have what we call "Big Table." Corporately, it's the best of what we do. It's a bit crazy creating a table big enough for two hundred people, but the experience of having food piled upon food, people moving about and sharing what they've made, is worth it. Unlike the potlucks of old, at the Big Table, communion is not a separate experience but is integrated with all the other food. Children and adults color with crayons while people sing and others tell their stories; it all happens while we feast and enjoy a small picture of heaven.

My friend Alan Hirsch e-mailed me just after New Year's in 2006 and said, "We had a great party, quite a mess, but lots of fun. Parties are sacrament to me." If the Puritans considered work to be as spiritual as singing hymns, then I think it's biblically fair to consider enjoying food together in the same sacred light. You may even take the Adullam challenge. One week do a Bible study with some Christian friends. The next week invite some non-Christian friends over or out for food. When it's done, see where you sensed God's presence the most. I think you'll find it was around the grub!

At a Saint Paddy's Day party in 2005, we had most of the church (about seventy-five people at the time) over to our house. Most were new to faith and to our context; they were used to parties, notwithstanding ours. We drank green beer, ate, and just sat around and had a great time. Earlier that day, I was at the ice rink with my daughters, and I saw a father of a girl who had joined my daughter's hockey team. The kids were becoming buddies, and I knew Hanna was coming over for the party, so I invited her dad, too. I didn't think he'd come, but he did, and as he came in I noticed that he was smuggling in a few beers in a cute little fanny pack. I took him outside to where all the pop and beer was stored in ice chests, and he laughed and said, "I brought my own. I figured a church party wouldn't be doing the normal green beer thing." Later that night, when I brought out the home brew that I'd been preparing all year, he really came out of his shell and met all the other people who were at the bar doing the taste test.

I'm not sure what definition you use for *evangelism*, but my favorite has to do with "changing people's assumptions." To me, if we can dismantle their stereotypes of Christians as glorified Amish or Quakers who only enjoy the intimacy of sex to make a child and whose only hobbies are doing puzzles together, we're on our way to helping them see the Kingdom in a new light. This is why having fun, enjoying life, and celebrating people, food, wine, art, music, recreation, and rest become so critical in seeing friends find God.

By the way, if you live like this, you might find that your kids will have fond church memories and grow to love the missional way of life.

Sharing Life

Sharing spontaneous life simply means being with each other in normal day-to-day existence. The key to this is the word *spontaneous*. This isn't rocket science, but we've come to realize that the compartmentalized approach to life, coupled with Americans' radical individualism, does make it hard for people to live incarnationally. When working with existing churches, we start with the assumption that even if people are in a small group or Bible study, they rarely see those people outside of those 90-minute get-togethers. Yes, people do enjoy life, recreation, and fun, but they usually do so to escape instead of sharing them with the people they are learning to love.

The power of sharing our lives with others is that we're more prepared for spontaneous interaction when God opens a door. You may remember the story in Acts 16 when Paul and a few of his buddies were heading out to pray. While en route, they were surprised to find a young girl following them, proclaiming their own message to others who were listening. Apparently she was annoying, and Paul eventually lost patience and, turning around, cast out the annoying demonic spirit that was toying with them. Notice the wording about this spontaneous situation: "It happened that as we were going to the place of prayer" (Acts 16:16; NASB).

I've concluded that, almost without exception, relationships are formed, important dialogue and conversation begin, and powerful moments of ministry occur during spontaneous, unplanned moments while we are sharing our lives together. In many cases, these events occurred when I didn't want to be some place or have someone with me. Over time, I have learned that "interruptions" are the very place where I look for God to work. It's almost as if God creates interruptions as his last attempt to get me out of my own life.

The next time you read through Matthew, Mark, Luke, and John, highlight every time something powerful happens between Jesus and people. You'll notice the majority of the stories happen in unplanned, interrupted moments. Most of Jesus' teaching was done "along the way" or "as they were going." What this means for us is that we must develop rhythms of sharing life so that these powerful moments can happen. If we only see ministry happening in our programmed world, according to our DayTimer, or in our church buildings, we'll continue to miss out.

○
———————

Reflection

○ What are the great good places in your community?

○ What would you have to change about your routine to become a "regular" there?

○ Come up with some of your own habits and rhythms. How can you apply creativity to your context?

———————
○

20

ONENESS

AS WE CONTINUE TO EXPLORE the habits and rhythms of incarnational church, this chapter may help those of you who are more shepherding in your orientation and who have been patiently waiting for us to talk about spiritual formation. Many leaders wonder if all this "community" and "mission" focus still allows for soul growth to happen.

Well, it does, and is dependent upon the spiritual vitality and depth of those on mission together. The Gospel of John is maybe the most beautiful story of a missionary son who lived among the world of sinners and yet was intimately connected to the Father. Jesus on several occasions mentioned how he only did what he saw his father doing. As he apprenticed his eventual "world changers," he taught them in Chapter 10 to be sheep that hear his voice; he called them in Chapter 14 to depend on the Holy Spirit for guidance. In Chapter 15 he changed to metaphor to being a branch that is connected to the vine and referenced the fact that apart from intimate knowledge and connection with him, they could accomplish nothing. In short, Jesus modeled a life commitment to be "out there" while apprenticing and modeling the need to be internally connected to the source of all mission.

When we say *communion*, this is what we are leaning into. The sphere of *communion* represents what we do to interact with God in worship, listening, and soul formation.

By now you've seen that the incarnational way of ministry changes our perspective on many aspects of church. With communion, we have to think a little outside the box as well.

Most of us learned to view communing with God as primarily happening in either a church worship service or in our own personal devotional time. A good majority of the transfer growth dilemma surrounds a systemic belief that corporate worship is the primary place God communes with us and we with him.

We think it's shortsighted and historically ignorant to assume that every time Christians met throughout history, they had a stage, trained singers, overheads, and well-choreographed vocal worship to help them connect with God. I've never found it that helpful to worship through singing, especially in front of people.

If worship were perfectly fitted to Hugh Halter, it would be a 5:30 a.m. moment, the sun peeking up over a grove of fresh-smelling pine trees, cool 45-degree air, my Copper Mountain coffee mug full of Seattle's Best coffee, and the sound of bagpipes echoing an ancient hymn over my outstretched fly rod. That would do it for me every time. But I doubt that's for everyone.

Matt and I would be the first to admit that instrument and voice worship is not our area of expertise. But we'd all be well served (if our goal is to reach culture) to look beyond our present forms of musical worship to include other ways of relating to God.

As we've now worked with hundreds of church planters and pastors who have been sensitively moving away from program- and presentation-based attempts to nurture the souls of their people, we've boiled it down to just a few things we think must always be present to connect with God.

In Adullam we share scripture, Sabbath gathering, and soulace space (represented in Figure 20.1).

Sharing Scripture

The most often-asked question after people come to our training or hear our story is, "Do you guys ever read the Bible?" I guess we give the impression that church is just one big Saint Paddy's Day party. We are here to admit that the scriptures are the center of our community and our congregational life. I know many of you are breathing a sigh of relief. Corporately, we simply walk through books of the Bible, together

Figure 20.1   Rhythms of Communion.

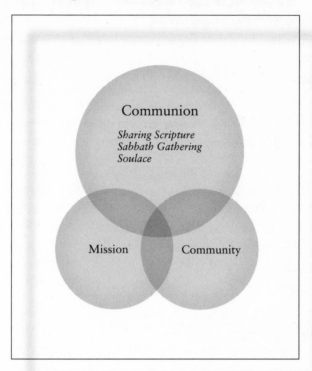

Communion

Sharing Scripture
Sabbath Gathering
Soulace

Mission   Community

our villages have the scriptures as a key part of what they share, and God's Word is at the center of our conversations with people who are trying to figure out Christ. And the first thing we do when a new person communicates he or she is curious is to buy that person a nice Bible.

The next questions we get are, "How can I grow deep with my Christian friends if a Sojourner comes into our community time? Don't they have different needs or interests? Wouldn't we have to 'dumb down' how we talk about God so they don't feel freaked out?"

To answer this, I'll take you to a training we did at a Bible-centered church.

We divided the attendants into two groups, one on each side of the room. The first side brainstormed a list of the things that Christians struggle with. The other side of the room put themselves in the mindset of a non-Christian and came up with a list of things that they, as non-Christians, would struggle with: vices, fears, relational issues, and so on. After about 10 minutes, we brought the groups together and had them compare notes. Guess what? There was no difference. Both Christians and Sojourners struggle with:

○ Marriage

○ Parenting

○ Doubting God

○ Trying to be a better person

○ Pornography

○ Materialism

○ Debt

○ Forgiving people who have sinned against them

○ Divorce

○ Sexual problems within marriage

○ Loneliness

○ Substance abuse

○ Alcohol

○ Marijuana use

○ Panic attacks

○ Relating with children

○ Anger issues

Why would you have to "dumb things down" for Sojourners? We're all the same. Sure, if we've come to know Christ and accept his message, we may be a few steps ahead in knowledge and transformation, and maybe even a bit ahead in getting out of vice, but I can't think of anything that would interest a nonbeliever that I also wouldn't love to talk about.

Remember, when a Sojourner comes into your community time or gathering, he or she will be there voluntarily, because the Sojourner wants to know what a Christian really is. He will already be a part of your people; she will feel as if she belongs with you; and most likely the person has a high level of trust and respect for your opinions. All that is left for you to do is to be honest. "Going deep" isn't about head knowledge or number of years following God. It's about honesty, common struggle, and being transparent in both weak and strong moments. (These are all things the evangelical tradition has taught us to hide or cover, not to divulge, which may be another reason Sojourners aren't beating our doors down. But that's another book.)

If you feel the need to lighten it up, you're ripping off both the Sojourner and yourself. Jesus never lightened up his message, even with the most far-out Sojourners, so we probably shouldn't either.

You might be asking, "What do you do, then, in regard to the Bible and discussion times?" Here's a simple habit your community can use around scripture that proves to be meaningful both to your Christians and to your Sojourners.

> Stretch out your right hand as far as you can. Next, measure the distance between your thumb and pinky. Read that much scripture only. Preferably a contained story or idea. Like the second chapter of James, or a parable, or one of the Psalms like Chapter 23.

> After you read the scripture, ask these five questions and let people answer as they feel led:

> 1. What did you like about what we just read?
> 2. What didn't you like?
> 3. Was there anything you didn't understand?
> 4. What did you learn about God?
> 5. Regardless of where your faith is at right now, if you were to apply what we learned about God to something in your life this week, what would that look like?

Seems pretty simple, maybe even shallow, but give it a shot. You'll notice some strangely deep dynamics that happen as a result of being in the scriptures together. And if your group is learning to be real, you'll be able to dive pretty deeply while also being relevant to any curious Sojourners who are with you. We suggest you use only scripture for this, because curriculum-based gatherings require a good facilitator or teacher, a lot of preparation by the leader, and much of the time feel quite unnatural. They also move linearly. That is, they usually build upon the previous discussion, so if new Sojourners join you in the middle of a three-month series, they'll feel lost or out of place. Keeping this simple grid around scripture allows you and your community to function without any preparation and will never create a sense of "in or out."

Sabbath Gathering

Does the term "Sabbath gathering" sound like "going to church"? It might, but there are some unique differences in how we process the idea of people gathering together for a common time of communion.

I was driving the other day and heard an announcer on a national Christian radio station say, "Remember, all Christians should be in church this Sunday." When I heard it, I found myself bristling with anger. As I pondered my reaction, I realized that we still think that's the end game for people. That is, if we just get people to church, everything else will take care of itself. Why did they have to challenge people to go? Why did I rarely want to go as I was growing up? It's an easy answer. The problem with church has been that we communicate that God is up in heaven, monitoring his cosmic seating chart, and he really wants our church buildings full.

That's just not true.

Church gatherings were never the intended goal; they were the natural result of people finding others who were living their alternative Kingdom story. The goal of our missional life is not to grow churches. The goal of church is to grow missionaries. The goal of the gospel is not to get people to church. The result of the gospel is that people will find each other and gather because of the deep meaning of a common experience.

In Hebrews 10:24–25, we have the only direct encouragement for people to gather: "And let us consider how we may spur one another on toward love and good deeds. Let us not give up meeting together, as some are in the habit of doing, but let us encourage one another." We must realize that this was not a plea for people to get their lazy fannies out of bed, put their Sunday paper down, postpone their family trip out to the lake, put on their Sunday best, and get to church. It was an encouragement for early Christians who feared for their lives, who were hiding in dark alleys, who were seeing their friends killed, and who weren't gathering because of great persecution. It was a plea for people to defy their fears and draw together with others who were living life in the margins of society, who were on a common mission, and who were in desperate need of being encouraged by the stories of others whose lives were in peril because of the gospel. People were naturally dispersed because of mission, and the gathering was their way to hear the faithful stories of others.

A couple of things can be learned from all this. First, mission creates meaning and a context for the gathering. In Adullam, we regularly communicate that we don't care if people come to a gathering. We focus on what they're doing "out there." We encourage people to use Sunday morning to be with Sojourners or use the time for benevolent action. We also stress that the deepest spiritual times should be experienced without our villages. When they take us up on the idea, they tell us that they missed the gathering. In other words, what used to be a "have to" or a "should do" becomes a "can't wait to."

The second thing that might be a switch is that when people are bent on mission first, the gathering takes on different purposes. We have found that when the primary values are outward mission and incarnational life, the gathering becomes more about connecting people, corporate storytelling, vision casting, and celebration. In settings where the church service is the main thing, Bible teaching, singing, prayer, and ministry to people becomes the priority. We prefer that Bible teaching, prayer, study, and ministry to people happen primarily in our communities during the week. I do feel it's important for God's voice to be heard through scripture in corporate settings, but we do this with a sense of God speaking vision into our collective mission rather than for personal self-help.

We're not anti-gathering; we just don't care how many people gather, or when, or for how long. We don't think smaller gatherings are better than larger gatherings. Our main focus is on *why* we gather and the meaning that is brought into our gathering due to our common story away from the gathering. This is why we encourage church planters not to start the church by launching a church service. Instead, we advocate that they launch people and add the gatherings as needed.

For an existing congregation, the challenge is to sensitively "not provide" things at the gathering that you want people to experience out in the world and slowly reestablish the meaning behind the weekly church service. Maybe, it shouldn't even be called a "service." That communicates, "You come here to get what you need."

Please hear what we're saying. We believe there is something very important about bringing people together. Humans have been doing this since the beginning of time, and if people are experiencing something that is meaningful to them, they'll want to invite others into their experience and you won't be able to hold them back. The key is to not let your gathering be more than it is supposed to be, nor to let people depend on the gathering for things it wasn't supposed to provide in the first place.

Soulace

The last habit we move people into is what we call "soulace" spaces. These are simple gatherings throughout the week where people can be together for a more communal experience in scripture, silence, prayer, and reflection.

Most of the soulace space is in a public zone, coffee shop, park, and so on. Sometimes they interact together and sometimes they just provide a space where people can be together in their personal time with God. I've heard of some that meet in a monastery and walk the stations of the cross together without talking. Others take a silent hike together and some just do a more traditional Bible study.

Whereas the Gathering provides the largest intersection for relational connection, celebration, and vision, and villages provide the most integrated opportunity for a group to be intentional with incarnational mission, soulace spaces create a web of spontaneous connections that provide for more soul growth. Soulace also seems to be an easier link into our villages and larger weekly gatherings together. They allow more flexibility for people to work around time constraints, and they provide a level of personal and communal spiritual formation that is sometimes missing in the larger corporate gatherings and villages.

In Chapter Twenty-One we complete the picture by addressing the *otherness* of mission.

O

Reflection

o Read Psalm 23 and answer the following questions:

- What did you like about what you just read?
- What didn't you like?
- Was there anything you didn't understand?
- What did you learn about God?
- Regardless of where your faith is tonight, if you were to apply what we learned about God to something in your life this week, what would that look like?

O

21

OTHERNESS

THIS LAST SPHERE OF incarnational community is the most fulfilling, the most fun, and the most inspiring and intriguing to the onlooking Sojourners. It's about *mission*.

A few weeks ago, the Adullam network enjoyed a great day of baptizing people in a lake close to Denver. It was our day to celebrate all the stories God has let us be a part of. One of the best stories was about Sean. Sean came to Denver to play professional lacrosse. He's a hard, rough Long Island guy, cut out of the *Braveheart* era. He ended up living with several of our guys who were leading a village, made up mostly of single urbanites. The village shared nearly everything: food, fun, friends and, of course, rent. One thing they didn't share, however, was their prayer time. Not only did they not want to freak Sean out, they didn't think he'd be interested.

One evening, however, before Sean sealed the deal with God, he taught us all a great lesson. While the group was praying for KC, a young girl who was heading up ministry to a needy community in Nicaragua, Sean broke into their silence and asked, "So, uh . . . what's going on in here?"

"We're praying for KC's trip down to Nicaragua to work in the dump," Lou responded. Thinking Sean would head back to his room, they were all surprised when he sat down with them and said in a deep

Figure 21.1   The Rhythms of Mission.

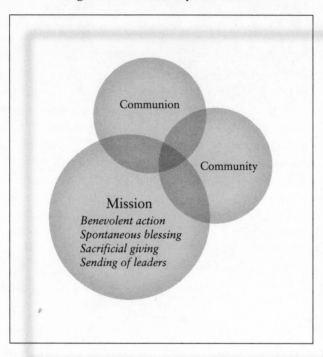

New York accent, "I think I'd like in on this!" Not only did he sit with them, he prayed his own unique blessing over KC.

Once again, you can see the beauty of people participating in deep Christian experiences even before they've come to faith. Christians often come into a church for communion; Sojourners more easily come in through community and mission.

In the sphere of mission, we ask people to share benevolent action, spontaneous blessing, sacrificial giving, and the sending out of leaders (as presented in Figure 21.1). But the essence of all these rhythms is participating in what God calls "pure" religion in James 1:27. It's taking care of orphans, widows, and the practical needs of a hurting world.

Benevolent Action

Several years ago, many churches were using a training manual that claimed to identify eight qualities of healthy churches and offered an assessment tool that could be used to find out how healthy your church was. Most denominations used it, and I even took our first church plant through it. Many of the categories were helpful, but people in our group began to notice that something was omitted. That is, there was no mention of *pure religion*, as James called it—selfless acts of benevolence primarily focused to the least, the poor, and the oppressed.

As Matt and I train church planters, we often ask, "What's going to be the unique thumbprint of God on your congregation? What is different about your calling than what God may call other churches to?"

Some say, "We're going to be a praying church." Some say, "I feel God has called us to be focused on those outside the church." Others say, "Our call is to take care of those in need." The point of the exercise is to help them understand their unique contribution. Although these three seem to come up the most, we have to sadly expose that none of them should be unique to any church. They are the common call of every church, anywhere in the world, in any era of time. All these, and especially the last, combine to form God's universal call to every local Body and believer.

In our church-being-planted, we took a few months and scoured all the scripture references that relate to the motive and focus of our faith; it accounted for roughly half of all the major themes of the Old and New Testament. The only themes larger are the messianic hope and the narratives about Christ. After that, everything points to God's redemption of the world, to injustice, poverty, and pain, with the Book of Revelation being the final redemption.

Mission gave Sean a place to feel involved in the Kingdom without even knowing God. Thus, mission is more than just doing good things for people. It's a primary means of helping people see what a Christian really is. Because this village had naturally integrated their mission with their community and their communion, they saw Sean make an extremely quick conversion to Christ.

You see, transformation is limited when all we do is write checks to global missions. True transformation happens only when God's heart becomes a habit in our normal Christian community. Mission is a natural part of everyone's discipleship, not of a fringe group in the church that focuses money and energy outside our normal programs. It's the easiest way to immediately make the concepts of God's loving Kingdom tangible to anyone.

In Adullam, each village chooses where they will live out their benevolence together. Some choose to pool their efforts into larger national or international efforts. They take regular trips to New Orleans or Nicaragua, each time using the mission as a spiritual formation exercise for those who are traveling. Some choose local Christian or secular needs-based initiatives, and some just decide to be available at a drop of a hat to rally their village and help someone with practical needs.

Sacrificial Giving

It is within the context of mission that we ask people to give of their resources. We don't mandate that they tithe, but we speak of the tithe optimistically and ask people to consider that a committed incarnational community has an incredible opportunity to help people. The tithe is part of the discipleship process to the whole person, but we understand that a tithe is not going to happen until someone's heart is touched. Jesus said it this way: "For where your treasure is, there your heart will be also" (Luke 12:34). We're finding that as we give freedom for people to use their money as God leads them, they begin to trust the larger Adullam network and increase their investment into God's corporate mission.

Many people outside and inside the church are skeptical of where church resources are going . . . and for good reason. When people give faithfully for years and never see a church extending benevolence or making a genuine impact in a community, it's quite natural to lose motivation. Yes, we should be able to trust our church leadership, but it's also okay to measure the way we use our corporate resources against how the ancient communities did. Why were they so jubilant about giving? Simply, they got to see it change lives!

Spontaneous Blessing

This focus on meeting needs leads our communities to look for ways to bless people spontaneously. As we said earlier, we do think that pooling our resources can be a great way to meet much larger needs that individuals can't handle on their own. But when you consider the idea of a church being a movement of benevolent action, it pushes us to consider how to make giving more natural, on time, and personal. The logical answer is that we must give permission and ownership for people and their communities to meet needs as they happen on the streets.

In our second year of Adullam, we were seeing only $4,000 to $5,000 a month coming into the community. Generally, we understood this to be normal based on our demographic of nonbelievers, new believers, and skeptical Christians, not to mention that we didn't take an offering during the gathering. Yet at other times, because I'm a normal pastor, I'd freak out internally about how much more we could do if we could just see more money flowing through our general fund. As Matt and I assessed the situation by talking to our village leaders, we realized that people were actually giving much more, but that their giving was meeting the needs of the people in their village or other practical needs of people outside our community.

If someone needed his car fixed, if someone couldn't pay a medical bill, if someone wanted to move out of a bad living situation, or if someone needed a plane ticket to get home to help with a family situation, people just pitched in and did what needed to get done to alleviate the *now* problem. Once Matt and I realized what was going on, we found great solace in knowing that God's heart was becoming the heart of our people.

Don't get me wrong, there's always a lot of room to help people excel more, and we wouldn't be able to give flight to spontaneous giving without some infrastructure funding. But we've learned that everything gets taken care of if you give people vision and permission to spend their money wisely on real people. So far, our general fund needs have always been sufficient to keep this practical needs co-op on the move.

This is a good time to ask some *what if* questions: What if every church was able to get every person to commit 5 percent of their income to the general church fund, but mobilized the other 5 percent to all the needs of their communities? How might that change how people view Christians? How can we give people more freedom and creativity in their giving? How do we help people's giving become more closely tied to their hearts?

Sending of Leaders

Finally, when we think about extending mission to the world, we again have to take the issue of leadership seriously. How are we going to meet all the social and practical needs of our neighborhoods, let alone our cities, without more leaders? Jesus, in Matthew 9:37–38, said, "The harvest is plentiful but the workers are few. Ask the Lord of the harvest, therefore, to send out workers into His field." His call to his church is to pray for, call out, and make a priority of sending more people into the world.

In Adullam, we prioritize putting money and time into developing leaders who can create new communities of blessing. Instead of putting a majority of the church's money into those things that fit in the category of communion (building, salaries, programs, curriculum), we put it into community and mission. Remember, whatever you give leadership to will grow. Equally, what you give your money and people to will grow. If you invest your finances in paid staff who provide a worship gathering, of course it should grow. If you give your money and time to leaders who help establish and oversee incarnational communities, then community and mission should grow.

As we summarize these habits and the spheres of what we refer to as the "Tangible Kingdom," we aren't trying to overload your already busy lives. We're trying to integrate them so that we all have more time to live—and live well. In most cases, we provide a monthly grid to help people get started. In a given month, each village commits one evening to a party at which they can share their friends, food, and fun. We ask them to commit one time to experiencing some aspect of mission, service, or benevolent action, and we suggest that a couple of times they gather as a community to open the scriptures, pray, and do anything that would help them commune with God. Rather than putting all the emphasis on communion, we find that the depth of relationships that forms by prioritizing the other two spheres (community and mission) helps to create a more meaningful experience for the missional people and the Sojourners.

There it is: easy, natural, meaningful, Tangible Kingdom community, with some baseline habits to begin to share together. Imagine the parts of the Kingdom that may open up to you if the same people you love to be with on Saturday night were the same people with whom you dive deep with spiritually. And then, in turn, they connect *their friends* with you and your friends.

Could be fun.

And it is.

o

Reflection

o What would need to change in your life (time and money) to be available for benevolent action, spontaneous blessing, or service to the community?

o

A DAY IN THE LIFE . . .

AS WE COME TO the end of this story, our hope is that we've given you a place to vent a little, repent a little, look beneath the surface of the water enough to understand where the church lost its way, and also have given you a glimmer of hope about finding God's Tangible Kingdom wherever you find yourself pitching your tent, as Jesus did.

I've heard that it's best to end a book with a really big bang. You know, an invitation so exciting that it leaves you, the reader, salivating for more. But because I'm not sure I want to relive the agony of writing again, and because I'd rather see you do less reading and more action, I thought it best to simply plop myself down at a local pub and reflect on my day.

Today was Sunday, and the day began with our Adullam gathering at a local community center. I was greeted by Earl, our mentally ill maintenance man, who was supposed to have all the chairs set up. Because of his obsessive compulsive disorder, he had gotten "locked up" cleaning the coffee pots over and over, so I helped him set up chairs while we talked about the ups and downs of bipolar meds. It may not sound like it, but it was a nice time.

Then, in came Jason, our worship facilitator. A better description is Jason, my friend, whom I look forward to seeing every Sunday morning. It's our time to catch up on the week and very rarely includes any discussion about how our worship gathering is going to go.

Next came in Sam, a twenty-two-year-old who simply loves Jesus and will do anything to serve. (Yep, they still exist!) Next came Nathaniel. He doesn't have any particular job on Sunday. He just comes because he likes to be with us. He usually helps make some coffee and eats a couple of blueberry donuts. If he doesn't show, I feel like something is missing.

About 10:00 a.m., more friends started to show up. Some brought other friends, some brought food to share, and some just came in. Our collective community is a strange mix of rednecks, professional athletes, Bronco cheerleaders, seminary students, young suburban couples, a herd of kids and babies, many single urbanites, and a handful of empty nesters who keep us in check. For the first 25 minutes, nobody sat down. Everyone just enjoyed waking up together with coffee, conversation, and the sound of our kids running all over. Then we shared some scripture, song, and communion, and one of our young interns told us about a mission to Zimbabwe and another to Nicaragua that we've all been drawn into.

I left with a sense that everyone was glad they had been together. As many followed Jason to the local pub where he plays on Sunday afternoons, I went home to watch the last round of the British Open.

As I settled into what I thought would be a five-hour "nap-golf extravaganza," the doorbell rang. It was Biker Lenny, asking if his friends (a local gang of pirates) could see our puppies. Now, I don't want you to miss this picture. Lenny and his friends, half of whom were women, have enough ink in their collective tattoos to overflow the printer cartridges for two hundred HP Office Jets. They all look like a cross between ZZ Top and Howard Stern, and that includes the ladies!

As we sat outside in our garage, some played with the puppies and the other ones looked over my Harley. Toward the end of our time, I got the invitation that I'd been asking God about for the past six months. They asked me to ride with them! Finally.

Thanks to the magic of TiVo and the leading of the Holy Spirit, I was able to leave the British Open and head off with Captain Jack Sparrow and his band of bikers to the thunderous sound of six Hogs—they in their black leather and bandanas, and me in my church shorts and flip-flops. As I proudly rode along, I had the strange feeling that I was being carried along into another Fiona story.

After the ride, thinking that my day was over, I headed to my local think spot to pen these words, only to be interrupted by a phone call from a couple who used to live next door to us. One of their daughters wanted to be baptized outside, and they couldn't find a church that would do this. Her mother had remembered us from a couple years back and found my number. I told her I'd be honored to baptize her daughter and invited them to our lakeside baptism gathering to be held a few weeks later.

This day sums up our hope for you. This day was just life as usual, and yet it was filled to the brim with beautiful expressions of God's Tangible Kingdom. Very little was planned, and the best parts came as divine interruptions to my normally self-focused life.

What we're learning is that God's church can be natural, and it will emerge anywhere an incarnational community exists. People will always be drawn to people who look, smell, and behave like Jesus, and if you're committed to caring for people who move toward Christ through you, church will become a labor of love for you, as well. Fresh faces, new stories, and a web of relationships will witness to the tangible world Jesus called his Kingdom.

As you let your hope rise up, you'll come to realize that the big picture Jesus spoke of when he talked of the Kingdom was never about "church." Church is simply a visible and invisible reality of what God does while we work with him in his redemptive ways in the world. God's church, therefore, is always around you, but it requires your participation to uncover and make tangible.

Please don't try to duplicate our story. We suggest you start by finding the Fionas in your world and love them until the Kingdom starts to unfold. If something noticeable happens . . . great! If not, then at least you're living out your faith in a way that will feel right to your soul and put a smile on God's face.

○

Final Reflection

○ What is church to you?

○ Are you ready to reengage and fight for the Tangible Kingdom?

○ Of the three spheres of Tangible Kingdom (community, communion, mission), which do you need to be the most intentional about developing in your life?

○

Now go set up a coffee time with your Fiona!
Hope to talk to you again someday.
Hugh & Matt

NOTES

The source for unattributed illustrations is D. L. Guder, ed., *Missional Church: A Vision for the Sending of the Church in North America*. Grand Rapids, Mich.: Eerdmans, 1998.

Chapter Two: Elvis Has Left the Building

1. The Barna Group, Ltd. "Twentysomethings Struggle to Find Their Place in Christian Churches." [http://www.barna.org]. September 24, 2003.
2. The Barna Group, Ltd. "Spirituality May Be Hot in America, But 76 Million Adults Never Attend Church." [http://www.barna.org]. March 20, 2006.
3. The Barna Group, Ltd. "Unchurched Population Nears 100 Million in the U.S." [http://www.barna.org]. March 19, 2007.
4. The Barna Group, Ltd. "Number of Unchurched Adults Has Nearly Doubled Since 1991." [http://www.barna.org]. March 4, 2004.
5. Tom Clegg and Warren Bird. *Lost in America*. Loveland, Colo.: Group Publishing, 2001, p. 27.
6. Ibid., p. 29.
7. Ibid., pp. 36, 57–58.
8. Baylor Religion Survey, p. 9.

Chapter Five: Moving Violations

1. *Webster's Dictionary*. Springfield, Mass.: Merriam-Webster, Inc.

Chapter Six: Posture

1. Brian D. McLaren. *More Ready Than You Realize*. Grand Rapids, Mich.: Zondervan, 2002.

2. Henri Nouwen. *Out of Solitude*. Notre Dame, Ind.: Ave Maria Press, 1974.

Chapter Eight: Paradigm

1. Josh McDowell. *Evidence That Demands a Verdict*. Nashville, Tenn.: Thomas Nelson, 1999.
2. Alan Hirsch. *The Forgotten Ways*. Grand Rapids, Mich.: Brazos Press, 2006, p. 62.
3. Diognetus, quoted by Robert Webber in Mike Yaconelli, ed., *The Door Interviews*. Grand Rapids, Mich.: Zondervan, 1989, pp. 212–213.

Chapter Nine: Jipped

1. Dallas Willard. *The Divine Conspiracy*. San Francisco, Calif.: HarperOne, 1998.
2. Tom Clegg and Warren Bird. *Lost in America*. Loveland, Colo.: Group Publishing, 2001, pp. 43–45.
3. Willard, *Conspiracy*, p. 15.

Chapter Twelve: Tip It Over

1. Dietrich Bonhoeffer. *Life Together: A Discussion of Christian Fellowship*. San Francisco, Calif.: HarperOne, 1954, p. 27.
2. Ernest Shackleton and the Endurance Expedition, Director Frank Hurley, 2002.

Chapter Seventeen: Loving Without Strings

1. Michael Frost and Alan Hirsch. *The Shaping of Things to Come*. Peabody, Mass: Hendrickson, 2003, p. 47.
2. Henri Nouwen. *Gracias!* New York: HarperCollins, 1983, pp. 147–148.

Chapter Eighteen: Inviting In

1. Mother Teresa. [www.brainyquote.com/quotes/authors/motherteresa]. Retrieved November 13, 2007.
2. The Barna Group, Ltd. [http://www.barna.org].

Chapter Twenty: Oneness

1. Ray Oldenburg. *The Great Good Place*. New York: Marlowe & Co., 1999.

THE AUTHORS

HUGH HALTER AND MATT SMAY are the national directors of Missio, a division of Church Resource Ministries (CRM) committed to apprenticing a global network of missional leaders, churches, and movements. They facilitate MCAP (Missional Church Apprenticeship Practicum), an international collaborative learning and training environment for incarnational leaders, church planters, and pastors. This Web-based practicum teaches pastors, church planters, and emerging leaders to innovate new forms of incarnational church. Hugh and Matt also co-lead Adullam, a church of incarnational communities in Denver, Colorado.

For more information on Missio/MCAP, visit http://www.missio.us or http://www.adullamdenver.com.

For *Tangible Kingdom: The Workbook*, other resources, and information on speaking and consulting opportunities, go to http://www.tangible kingdom.com.

CRM EMPOWERING LEADERS

CRM (Church Resource Ministries; www.CRMleaders.org) is a movement committed to developing leaders to strengthen and multiply the Church worldwide.

Over 300 CRM missionaries live and minister in nations on every continent, coaching, mentoring, and apprenticing those called to lead and serve the Christian movement in their settings. This results in the multiplication of godly leaders who have a passion for their world and who are empowered to multiply their lives and ministry. Through them, CRM stimulates movements of fresh, authentic churches, holistic in nature, so that the name of God is renowned among the nations.

INDEX

A

Acts 2, 148–149
Acts 5:1–11, 52–53
Acts 5:13, 50
Acts 11:1–18, 54
Acts 16, 161
Acts 19, 61
Acts, Book of, 69
Adullam: and benevolent action, 173–174; "Big Table" event and, 88–89, 160; and communion, 164–170; and Discovery Zone, 65–66; and incarnational communities, 149–150; and incarnational model, 96; and individualism, 151; main gathering of, 104–105; membership process of, 91; and modeling missional life, 109–110; network of, 42; origin of, xx–xxi; and Sabbath gathering, 168–169; and sending of leaders, 175; and spontaneous blessing, 174–175; values of, 54–55; and visitors, 113–114
Advocacy, and missionaries, 43–46
Ancient church: and community, 70–71; and leaving habit, 128; as pre-institutional, 50–55; and relationships, 69; values of, 74–75. *See also* Gospel response
Annanias, 52–53
Apprenticeship, 97
Attractional church model: and correcting people, 53; nature of, 93–94; and pyramid structure, 102–106
Autonomy, 67–69

B

Baby boomers, as unchurched, 13
Barna Group, 9, 11–12, 154
Baylor Religion Survey, 12
Belief, approaches to, 64–67
Benevolent action, as aspect of mission, 172–174
Bible. *See* Scripture; *specific books*
Biblical confrontation, 52–53
"Big Table" event, in Adullam, 88–89, 160
Bird, W., 12
Blessing, concept of, 89, 142–145, 174–175
Bonhoeffer, D., 112

C

Castaway (film), 23
Christendom church, after Constantine, 55–57
Christology, 20–21
Church attendance statistics, 9, 11–12
The Church Between Gospel and Culture: The Emerging Mission in North America (Hunsberger and Van Gelder), 103, 110, 114, 117
Church growth, and transfers, 12–13
Church Resource Ministries, 4
"Circling the Wagons" concept, 30
Civil war, and churches, 18–21
Clegg, T., 12
Communication, importance of nonverbal type, 39–43
Communion, 128, 148–150, 163–170
Community: in incarnational community, 148–150, 157–162;

Community: (*continued*)
  inclusive type of, 54–55, 70–72;
  need for, 87; sacrificial type of, 52
Confrontation, value of, 52–53
Constantine, 50–57, 102
Consumerism, 54–55, 111–112,
  151–153
Conversions, lack of, 12, 14
1 Corinthians 5:9, 45
1 Corinthians 6:9, 44, 45
1 Corinthians 9:20–23, 136–137
1 Corinthians 10:23–31, 136
1 Corinthians 11:17–34, 128
1 Corinthians 15:19, 74
2 Corinthians 5:16, 133
Correction, of people, 53
Cultural distance concept, 72

D

Deconstruction, and Postmodernism,
  76
Deuteronomy 5, 89
Deuteronomy 6:18, 89
Diognetus, 75
Discovery Zone, and gospel response,
  65–67, 95
The Divine Conspiracy (Willard), 84,
  90
Doctrine, and Jerusalem Christians,
  19–20
"Doing Church Differently" concept,
  29–30

E

Easternism: and belief, 64; definition
  of, 62–63; and influence, 76; and
  relationships, 69; and success
  measurement, 79; values of, 73–74
Ecclesiastes 3:11, 74
Ecclesiology, 20–21
Elway, J., 7, 25
Emergent churches, nature of, 13–14
Empathy, nature of, 44

The Enlightenment, 61–62
Ephesians 2:12, 148
Eternity now concept, value of, 74–75
Evangelism, 41–47, 160
Evidence That Demands a Verdict
  (McDowell), 64

F

Food, sharing of in incarnational
  community, 159–161
The Forgotten Ways (Hirsch), 72
Friends, sharing of in incarnational
  community, 157–159
Frost, M., 144

G

Galatians 5:17, 149–150
Galilee Christians, 19–21
Genesis 12:1–3, 142
Genesis 12:2, 89
Gesundheit Institute, 123
Gibbs, E., 28
Gospel, nature of, 84–91
Gospel response: and belief, 65–67,
  95; definition of, 63; and influence,
  76–78; and relationships, 70–72;
  and success measurement, 79–81;
  values of, 74–75
Gratification, value of, 74
The Great Good Place (Oldenburg),
  157
Growth. *See* Church growth

H

Haggard, T., 30–31
Hebrews 10:24–25, 168
Hebrews 12:1, 25
Heresy, 71
Hierarchy, 75–76
Hirsch, A., 72, 144, 160
Holiness, issue of, 135–140
Holistic view, of Easternism, 69

Homeschooling, 73, 136
Hunsberger, G. R., 103, 110, 114, 117

I

Incarnational church model: concept of, 38–39; and correcting people, 53; leadership in, 108–112; nature of, 95–99; and neomonastic church, 112–116; and Sojourners, 116–121. *See also* Living out process
Incarnational community: barriers to, 150–154; spheres of, 147–150
Inclusive community, 54–55, 70–72, 104
Individualism, 67–69, 150–151
Industrial Revolution, 62
Influence, nature of, 75–78
Institutions, and influence, 75–76
Inviting in process, and incarnational community spheres, 147–150
Isaiah 61:1–2, 89–90

J

James 1:27, 172–173
James 2:14–17, 142
Jerusalem Christians, 19–21
Jesus: attraction of, 46; and blessing, 142–143; and disciples, 118–119; in Gospel of John, 163; and holiness, 138, 139–140; and listening, 133; and living out, 125; and reason for coming, 89–90; and woman caught in adultery, 44–46
John 5:39, 20
John 6:54, 114
John 6:67, 27, 114–115
John 8, 44–46
John 14:6–8, 119
John 17:15, 140
1 John 2:6, 136
1 John 4:18, 71
John, Gospel of, 163

Judas, 119
Justification, and success measurement, 79

K

Kennedy, J. F., 63
Kennedy, R. F., 63
King, M. L., Jr., 63
Kingdom values, 51–55

L

Leadership: in incarnational church model, 108–112; nature of, 75–78; and sending of leaders, 175–176
Leaving, as habit of living out, 127–130
Legacy, and Easternism, 73–74
Life, sharing of in incarnational community, 161–162
Life Together (Bonhoeffer), 112
Listening, as living out habit, 131–133
Living among, as living out habit, 135–140
Living out process: and leaving as habit of, 127–130; and listening as habit of, 131–133; and living among as habit of, 135–140; nature of, 124
Lost, concept of, 40
Lost in America (Clegg and Bird), 87
Luke 4:18–19, 89–90
Luke 9:58–60, 114
Luke 12:34, 174
Luke 14:28–30, 116

M

Mark 1:15, 89
Mark 8:35, 142
Materialism, as barrier to incarnational community, 153–154
Matthew 5:13, 14, 136
Matthew 8:20–22, 27

Matthew 9:36, 46
Matthew 9:37–38, 175
McDowell, J., 64
McLaren, B., 40
Missiology, 20–21
Mission, in incarnational community, 148–150, 171–176
Missional Church Apprenticeship Program (MCAP), 18–19
Missional church model. *See* Incarnational church model
Missional structure, of incarnational church model: leadership in, 108–112; and neomonastic church, 112–116; and Sojourners, 116–121
Missionality, degrees of, 34–36
Missionaries, 38–39, 43–46
Modeling, and Gospel response, 76–78
Modernism. *See* Westernism/Modernism
More Ready Than You Realize (McLaren), 40
Mother Teresa, 151

N

Neomonastic church, 112–116
Nonconversions, 11
Nonverbal communication, importance of, 39–43
Nouwen, H., 44, 144–145

O

Oldenburg, R., 157
Oneness, in incarnational community, 148–150, 163–170
Otherness, in incarnational community, 148–150, 171–176

P

Paradigm, concept of, 59–61

Paradigms. *See* Easternism; Gospel response; Postmodernism; Westernism/Modernism
Patch Adams (film), 123–125
Paul, Apostle, and posture concept, 41–42
1 Peter 3:15, 42
Pew sitters, 113–114
Pharisee-ism, 19
Pharisees, and woman caught in adultery, 44–46
Planters, 33–36
Pluralism, and Postmodernism, 70
Postmodernism: and belief, 64; definition of, 63; and influence, 76; and relationships, 70; and success measurement, 79; values of, 74
Posture, concept of, 39–43
Pre-Constantine church, 50–55
Process, and success measurement, 79
Product, and success measurement, 78–79
Proverbs 15:1, 41
Pure religion concept, 172–173
Pyramid structure: in attractional church model, 102–106; in incarnational church model, 107–121

R

Relationships, approaches to, 67–70
Relevant churches. *See* Emergent churches
Rules, of life, 112

S

Sabbath gathering, 167–169
Sacrificial community value, 52
Sacrificial giving, as aspect of mission, 174
Saphira, 52–53
Sceva, seven sons of, 61

Scripture: sharing of in incarnational community, 164–167. *See also specific books*

Security, and Westernism/Modernism, 73

Sending, of leaders, 175–176

September 11, 2001, 62

Settlers, 33–36

Shackleton, E., 115–116

The Shaping of Things to Come (Hirsch and Frost), 144

Shepherds, 33–36

Short-sheeted gospel, 84–88

Significance, need for, 87

Sojourners, 116–121

Soulace space, 169–170

Spontaneous blessing, 174–175

Structure of church, 102–106

Success, measurement of, 78–79, 105

Surveys, 9, 11–12

T

Ten Commandments, 89

Tension, sources of, 16–22

1 Thessalonians 2:7–8, 41

Tithe, 174

Togetherness, as community, 148–150, 157–162

Traditional-attractional church model. *See* Attractional church model

Traditions, and Easternism, 76

Transcendence, need for, 87

Transfer growth, 12–13

Transformation, and success measurement, 79–81, 98

Truth, concept of, 41–42

Two-coffee rule, 78–79

Two-visit rule, 54–55

U

Unchurched, number of, 11–12, 13

Unworthy communion, 128

V

Values, approaches to, 72–75

Values, of Kingdom, 51–55

Van Gelder, C., 103, 110, 114, 117

Vietnam War, 63

Visionary churches. *See* Emergent churches

W

Westernism/Modernism: and belief, 64–65; definition of, 61–62; and influence, 75–76; and relationships, 67–70, 150–151, 153–154; and success measurement, 78–79; values of, 73

Whimsical holiness, 136, 138–140

Willard, D., 84

Woman caught in adultery story, 44–46

World Trade Center, 62

Building a Healthy Multi-Ethnic Church:
Mandate, Commitments, and Practices of a Diverse Congregation

Mark DeYmaz

Cloth
ISBN13: 978-0-7879-9551-5

"The Mosaic Church of Central Arkansas is influencing a systemic rethinking of things and setting an example that few churches to date have been willing to address."
—**From the preface by U.S. Senator Mark L. Pryor**

"We cannot ignore the topic of multi-ethnic churches as we live in a multi-ethnic world. Mark DeYmaz writes [with] practical insight, not from theory but from leading an extremely strategic multi-ethnic church that is paving the way for so many others."
—**Dan Kimball, senior pastor, Vintage Faith Church, Santa Cruz, California, and author, *They Like Jesus But Not the Church***

"This book unpacks theological and practical principles for local churches interested in truly serving their neighboring communities in an increasingly diverse America. It paves the way for the future of the local church and the next generations of its leaders."
—**D. J. Chuang, director, Asian American Church Research at Leadership Network and executive director at L[2] Foundation**

Building a Healthy Multi-Ethnic Church explains why the growing fascination with multi-ethnic churches must not be focused on racial reconciliation but on reconciling individuals to Jesus Christ and on reconciling local congregations of faith with the inclusive nature of the New Testament Church. Through personal stories and a thorough analysis of the biblical text, Mark DeYmaz, pastor of one of the most proven multi-ethnic churches in the country, provides the theological mandate for the multi-ethnic church and outlines seven core commitments required to bring it about. Writing from his comprehensive experience in planting, growing, and encouraging more ethnically diverse communities of faith, he demonstrates why the most effective way to advance the Gospel in the twenty-first century will be through strong and vital multi-ethnic churches.

Mark DeYmaz is pastor of the Mosaic Church of Central Arkansas, a multi-ethnic and economically diverse church where men and women from more than thirty nations currently worship God together as one. Formerly he served on Little Rock's Racial and Cultural Diversity Commission and he is a cofounder of the Mosaix Global Network, an organization dedicated to enlisting and equipping leaders intent on the development of multi-ethnic churches throughout America and beyond.

Church Unique:
How Missional Leaders Cast Vision, Capture Culture, and Create Movement

Will Mancini
Foreword by Max Lucado

Cloth
ISBN13: 978978-0-7879-9683-3

"What if God has the vision for your church? What if it is just for you? What if He wants you to know it? If you've answered yes to those questions then *Church Unique* is a book for you. Will Mancini has done us all a great favor in releasing the practical ways he helps church leaders envision their own unique future. His insights provide you the coaching you need to prepare you for your next ministry chapter."
—**Reggie McNeal**, author of *Practicing Greatness* and *The Present Future*

Written by church consultant Will Mancini, an expert on a new kind of visioning process to help churches develop a stunningly unique model of ministry that leads to redemptive movement. He guides churches away from an internal focus to emphasize participation in their community and surrounding culture. In this important book, Mancini offers an approach for rethinking what it means to lead with clarity as a visionary. Mancini explains that each church has a culture that reflects its particular values, thoughts, attitudes, and actions and shows how church leaders can unlock their church's individual DNA and unleash their congregation's one-of-a-kind potential.

Will Mancini (Houston, Texas) is a former pastor and the founder of Auxano, a national consulting group that works with traditional and emerging churches and ministries of all types around the country to help leaders to do a more visionary form of strategic planning. Some prominent clients include Chuck Swindoll's Stonebriar Community Church; Discovery Church in Orlando, led by David Loveless (who recently received honorable mention in the "Fifty Most Influential Pastors" article by Church Report); Ronnie Floyd's First Baptist Springdale and The Church at Pinnacle Hills with 9000 members; and best-selling author Max Lucado's church.

Organic Church:
Growing Faith Where Life Happens

Neil Cole
Foreword by Leonard I. Sweet

Cloth
ISBN13: 978-0-7879-8129-7

"This book is profound, practical, and a pleasure to read. It stretches our thinking and brings us to a place where we can see the Kingdom of God spread across the world in our generation. This book has come at the right time."
—**John C. Maxwell, founder, INJOY, INJOY Stewardship Services and EQUIP**

"I heartily recommend this book. It is packed with deep insights; you will find no fluff in it. Among the books on church planting, it offers a rare combination of attributes: it is biblical and well written, its model has proven effective, and it is authored by a practitioner rather than an observer or an ivory-tower theoretician."
—**Curtis Sergeant, directory of church planting, Saddleback Church**

Churches have tried all kinds of ways to attract new and younger members - revised vision statements, hipper worship, contemporary music, livelier sermons, bigger and better auditoriums. But there are still so many people who aren't being reached, who don't want to come to church. And the truth is that attendance at church on Sundays does not necessarily transform lives; God's presence in our hearts is what changes us. Leaders and laypeople everywhere are realizing that they need new and more powerful ways to help them spread God's Word. According to international church starter and pastor Neil Cole, if we want to connect with young people and those who are not coming to church, we must go where people congregate. Cole shows readers how to plant the seeds of the Kingdom of God in the places where life happens and where culture is formed - restaurants, bars, coffeehouses, parks, locker rooms, and neighborhoods. *Organic Church* offers a hands-on guide for demystifying this new model of church and shows the practical aspects of implementing it.

Visit the Leadership Network Website, www.leadnet.org, for more innovative resources and information. You can find more resources on organic church planting at www.cmaresources.org

Neil Cole is a church starter and pastor, and founder and executive director of Church Multiplication Associates, which has helped start over seven hundred churches in thirty-two states and twenty-three nations in six years. He is an international speaker and the author of Cultivating a Life for God.

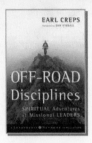

Off-Road Disciplines
Spiritual Adventures of Missional Leaders

Earl Creps
Foreword by Dan Kimball

Cloth
ISBN13: 978-0-7879-8520-2

"As a well-traveled explorer of the Church over many years, Earl offers more than a description of the latest cool topics in leadership. . . . You hold something that is rich, cured, and aged to sink into your mind and heart in a way that couldn't happen without breadth of experience behind it. This isn't a book about a quick fix to break an attendance barrier, or bringing new music or a new design for a worship gathering. It isn't about how to give better sermons. Earl writes about the most important thing he has discovered in all his exploring of the Church: the life of the missional leader and its effect on a missional organization."

—from the Foreword by Dan Kimball

In *Off-Road Disciplines*, Earl Creps reveals that the on-road practices of prayer and Bible reading should be bolstered by the other kinds of encounters with God that occur unexpectedly—complete with the bumps and bruises that happen when you go "off-road." Becoming an off-road leader requires the cultivation of certain spiritual disciplines that allow the presence of the Holy Spirit to arrange your interior life. Earl Creps explores twelve central spiritual disciplines—six personal and six organizational—that Christian leaders of all ages and denominations need if they are to change themselves and their churches to reach out to the culture around them.

Earl Creps explores each of these off-road disciplines and shows how to make them part of normal daily life so that they can have a transformative effect. Creps provides a map of the cultural terrain leaders must navigate and offers insight on the ways in which the process of personal spiritual formation can lead to changes in organizations.

Visit the Leadership Network Website, www.leadnet.org, for more information.

Earl Creps—a popular speaker and leader—is director of the Doctor of Ministry program and associate professor at the Assemblies of God Theological Seminary (AGTS) in Springfield, Missouri. He has been a pastor, ministries consultant, and university professor. Along the way, Creps earned a Ph.D. in communication at Northwestern University and a doctor of ministry degree in leadership at AGTS.